595.789
G647a   Goode, Mark Richard
                 An introduction to Costa Rican Butterflies /
             Mark Richard Goode. -- 1a. ed. -- San José,
C.R.

                 : M.R. Goode, 1999.
                  98 p. il byn. algs. col. ; 14 x 22 cm.

ISBN 9977-12-365-9

             1. Mariposas - Costa Rica - Guías. I. Título.

AN INTRODUCTION TO COSTA RICAN

Butterflies

MARK RICHARD GOODE

AN INTRODUCTION
TO COSTA RICAN BUTTERFLIES

CONTENTS

FOREWORD

This book was created in order to provide a simple reference which will enable individuals to develop an appreciation for the diverse variety of butterflies to be found in Costa Rica. Its content and scope is intended to cater to those whose interest in butterflies is just beginning. What is presented is a basic, but informative overview relating to the ecology and habits of some of Costa Rica's most familiar and interesting butterflies.

It is the author's sincere hope that this book will provide the reader with the stimulation necessary to develop a deeper and lasting personal interest in these beautiful and precious creatures, and also of the rapidly diminishing habitats in which they live. The existing jeopardy in which human activities place the natural world should be of concern to everyone.

In particular, the beleaguered rainforests that exist in Costa Rica and elsewhere, and the astonishing variety of life that resides within them, must be urgently preserved. This gesture would not only be of benefit to future generations, but would serve as well to bestow a basic measure of dignity to all of the life that shares this planet with humanity. Countries such as Costa Rica would be much the poorer for the lack of the beautiful blue Morpho butterflies which sail gracefully through its lush and mysterious forests. Sights such as these are surely worth protecting simply for their own sake.

Mark Goode

PREFACE

The butterflies of Costa Rica provide both the resident and traveller with a fascinating and colourful insight into the ecology of a country which is small in area, yet as rich as any in the world from the viewpoint of biodiversity. These insects exist in all of the varied habitats which are present in Costa Rica, and exhibit specializations in structure, colouration and behaviour that could readily fill many lifetimes of study. For the motivated individual, a wonderful opportunity exists with regard to learning more about the interrelationships that these marvelous creatures have with the rest of Costa Rica's rich natural heritage.

Butterflies are by design a conspicuous and generally accessible subject to study in an ecological context. It is often surprising how much insight may be gained in relation to these creatures simply by the means of making careful observations while visiting their habitats. This book is intended to provide simple guidance to anyone who wishes to embark upon such a journey of discovery. What follows is a short synopsis of the different subject areas which are covered in this guide.

What are Butterflies?

In order to provide an answer to this question, details which pertain to the origins and physical structures of butterflies are related to the reader. In addition, the different stages that must be completed in order for metamorphosis to be achieved are discussed, as well as factors which may prohibit their development, such as the afflictions dealt to them by a variety of parasites and predators.

Mimicry and Sexual Dimorphism in Butterflies

The fascinating phenomenon of mimicry in butterflies is introduced, and the purpose behind the duplication of the colours and patterns of inedible species of butterflies by different related or non-related edible varieties is explained. Visual examples are also provided, in order to convey this important concept clearly to the reader.

Scientific Terminology

The scientific terminology which is utilized in order to accurately classify and identify butterflies and other organisms is discussed, with regard to its origins and current applications. This will enable the reader to appreciate the relevance of such terms, and allow the use of correct scientific names to be possible while studying butterflies in the field. The utilization of scientific names is furthered in this section by the means of an outline which provides details pertaining to the distinctiveness of the different families and subfamilies of butterflies which occur in Costa Rica.

Different Habitats in Costa Rica

An overview is provided which relates to the many different habitats that exist in Costa Rica, and the most productive areas within them that may be surveyed for butterflies. Also mentioned are details pertaining to the familiar species of butterflies that may be expected to be encountered in each particular habitat. Additionally, the visitor to Costa Rica is supplied with suggestions as to possible localities that they may wish to explore for butterflies.

How and Where to Find Butterflies in Costa Rica

The reader is given simple and helpful advice with regard to locating a variety of butterfly species within any given habitat. These suggestions are based upon approaches which have been practiced successfully by the author, in order to enhance his observations of many species of butterflies. Further information is conveyed to the reader regarding the habits of species which may be of particular interest to the enthusiast, such as those of *Morpho* butterflies.

Individual Species Accounts

This section provides colour photographs, which are cross referenced to individual species accounts that provide information pertaining to some of Costa Rica's most familiar and interesting butterflies. The species accounts enlighten the reader as to the distribution, larval foodplants, and life histories of these butterflies, and are based upon personal observations that the author has made in the field.

Butterfly Farming

Commercial butterfly farming in Costa Rica is discussed. The reader is informed as to the methods which are utilized in order to raise and subsequently export butterflies from Costa Rica, from the perspectives of both the breeder and exporter.

Glossary

A comprehensive glossary is offered for reference purposes. This resource will quickly enlighten the reader as to the meanings of a variety of new terms that will be encountered while using this book.

Checklist

Finally, a checklist which includes all of the butterflies that are dealt with in the species accounts is provided. Species which are observed while the reader is in the field may be checked off as they are seen. In addition, information relating to the habits and behaviours of the many different butterflies which are encountered by the reader may be recorded upon the extra pages which are provided after the checklist for the purposes of note taking.

ACKNOWLEDGEMENTS

I would like to thank some of the many wonderful people who have strongly encouraged my pursuits with butterflies. Firstly my parents Margaret and Albert, who have endured many years that have been perpetually filled with butterflies and caterpillars. Prof. Patrick Blandin, of the Museum National D'Histoire Naturelle (Paris) who has shared his valuable time with me, and in the process has increased my enthusiasm for the study of *Morpho* butterflies. Mr.Ken Thorne of Lambeth, Ontario, Canada for his valued friendship and assistance. Mr and Mrs Rod Parrott, of Port Hope, Ontario, Canada who kindly invited me to their home upon many occasions, and have done much to encourage my interests in butterflies . Mr. Gilles Deslisle, of St. Raymond, Quebec, Canada, for his kind assistance, and for providing me with materials for study. Mr. Raymond Murphy of Torquay, Devon, England, for sharing his personal insights and information relating to the butterflies of many lands.

Finally, I would like to thank my wife Roxana for her love and constant support during the development of this book. She patiently tolerated my obsessive behaviour at times, and accompanied me on numerous journeys into the wilds of Costa Rica, in order to gather necessary information. All of my love for everything that you have helped me to accomplish, and that friendly but firm finger that kept poking me along at times.

Mark Goode

CHAPTER I

WHAT ARE BUTTERFLIES?

Butterflies belong to the insect order Lepidoptera, which is comprised of about 170,000 species, including moths. Lepidoptera have been discovered in the fossil record from as long ago as 130 million years, and are thought to have blossomed and evolved as a result of the appearance and diversification of flowering plants.

Generally speaking, butterflies possess club-tipped antennae, whereas moths usually lack these features, and instead exhibit antennae which are more intricate in design, sometimes being very large and feather in appearance. These structures serve as extremely effective detectors of pheromones; chemical scents which the females of many species of butterflies and moths produce and disseminate in order to attract mates. Moths usually confine their activities to the nighttime, while most butterflies prefer to fly during the day.

Butterflies and moths share the same basic physical structures as many other types of insects such as bees, wasps and beetles, and have evolved over countless millennia into one of the most diverse and specialized groups of creatures in existence. When delving into the realm of these insects, one quickly learns to appreciate the astonishing variety of shapes, colours, and the infinite array of behaviours that butterflies have developed. This leaves one with the impression that these insects have few rivals as far as adaptations are concerned.

The word Lepidoptera is a latin term, which simply means "scale-winged." This description refers to the minute scales which clothe the wings and bodies of these insects, and serve to provide the unique colours, patterns and textures of each species that we encounter. These scales are arranged upon the wings of the insect in a manner similar to that of shingles upon a roof.

The colours of the scales may be produced by pigments, or alternatively by the means of microscopic structuring upon the scales themselves. In the latter case, hundreds of thousands of miniature prisms may be created, which are capable of producing a dazzling variety of metallic colours, depending upon the species in question. Species of butterflies which exhibit structural wing colouration include the famous blue *Morpho* butterflies (Morphinae).

The males of many butterflies often possess specialized wing scales which are referred to as androconia. These convey chemicals which serve to stimulate, and sometimes placate prospective mates while courtship ensues. Androconial scales may take the form of long, hair-like structures, brush-like plumes, or loosely attached structures that may be released in the manner of a powder.

The Structure of a Butterfly

The body of an adult butterfly is subdivided into three main sections: the head, Thorax and abdomen (Fig. 1.1).

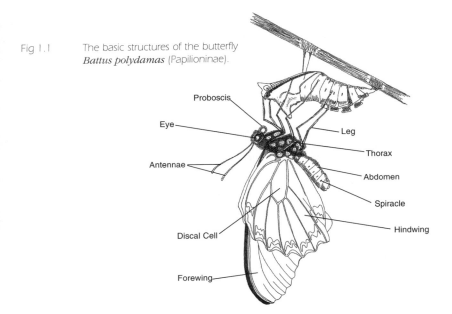

Fig 1.1   The basic structures of the butterfly
Battus polydamas (Papilioninae).

Proboscis

Eye

Leg

Thorax

Antennae

Abdomen

Spiracle

Discal Cell

Hindwing

Forewing

The Head

The head of a butterfly (Fig. 1.1) bears its sensory and feeding structures. Most conspicuous amongst the features of the head are two large, compound eyes, a pair of antennae (which are usually "club-tipped" in most species of butterflies), and a coiled proboscis, or "tongue", which is extended in order for the butterfly to consume its liquid food sources.

The Thorax

Adjacent to the head is the thorax (Fig. 1.1), which bears four wings and six legs. It also houses the muscles which enable the butterfly to take flight. The thorax is divided into three segments, with the wings being attached to the most posterior pair.

Butterflies possess six articulated legs, which vary in respect to their structure from family to family within the order Lepidoptera. In the case of the majority of butterflies, the first pair of legs are reduced in size, and are not functional for walking; these being used primarily by the female when searching for potential larval hostplants. Different plants are tested for suitability by the means of the female "drumming" these stumpy forelegs upon the surfaces of the leaves until a suitable plant is located.

The Wings

Each wing of a butterfly consists of two fused membranes, which are supported by a framework of thin and rigid veins (Fig. 1.1). These veins are extremely variable in configuration, and provide a convenient way of classifying different families and genera of butterflies.

As mentioned previously, the wings are covered in minute scales which are either pigmented or structurally designed to express an enormous variety of colours. Anyone who has handled a butterfly will have noticed that "powder" is left upon one's fingers if the wings are touched. This powder is actually composed of thousands of scales, which have been dislodged in the process of examining the insect.

It is a common misconception that butterflies are unable to fly if they lose even a small quantity of their wing scales. Butterflies can fly very effectively even when large portions of their wings have been removed, due to attempted predation.

The Abdomen

The final section of a butterfly's body is its abdomen (Fig. 1.1), which is segmented and quite flexible in comparison to its other body sections. Located within the abdomen is the digestive tract, and upon it, the external reproductive structures, which are visible at its tip.

Butterfly males exhibit two plate-like features upon the terminal abdominal segment, which are referred to as claspers. These claspers serve to securely grip the abdomen of the female while mating ensues. Female butterflies possess different organs at the same location on their abdomens, of which the primary one is referred to as the ovipositor. It is through the ovipositor that fertile eggs are passed, and then deposited upon the plants which will serve as hosts to the subsequent larvae. The process of egg-laying itself is called oviposition.

Many species of butterflies possess specialized glands upon their abdomens which produce a wide variety of pheromones; chemical scents which are recognizable to individuals of like species. These scents may often be very apparent even to the human nose. Those of *Morpho* species are quite reminiscent of vanilla. In the case of the latter butterflies, the pheromones are released from brush-like structures, which are extended from the abdomen of the male during courtship.

Glands may also be present which exude noxious odours that are utilized by many butterflies as a means of chemical defense. This serves to deter birds and other predators from eating the butterflies in question. Many species of *Heliconius* butterflies (Heliconiinae) utilize this form of protection, which in their case is released from eversable, fleshy nodes that are popularly referred to as "stink clubs". The different odours that are produced may often provide a reliable method of discriminating between many confusingly similar species.

Metamorphosis: The Life Cycle of a Butterfly

All butterflies must pass through three distinctive stages of development in order to become a mature insect, namely the egg, larva and pupa. This method of growth is referred to as a COMPLETE METAMORPHOSIS, the latter word meaning "change of form". This term is extremely accurate, as all of these stages are totally dissimilar from each another. One may not realize that an often unattractive caterpillar, which might possibly be ignored, could eventually produce a gloriously coloured butterfly.

The Egg

All butterflies begin their lives as an egg, or ovum, which is usually deposited upon the hostplant that the young larva will feed upon when it hatches. The eggs of butterflies exhibit a great degree of diversity with regard to their structure (Fig. 1.2), although those most commonly encountered are spherical, urchin, bottle or barrel shaped. They may be textured in a variety of different ways, such as being smooth, ribbed, honeycombed, or sometimes covered with an intricate array of minute spines.

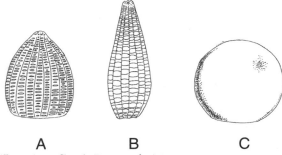

A   **B**   **C**

Fig 1.2   Eggs of different butterflies. A: *Danaus plexippus*;
B: *Phoebis philea*; C: *Papilio anchisiades*.

Butterfly eggs are tiny, with the majority being under 1.5 millimeters in general dimensions. When initially deposited, the eggs are usually white, yellowish or greenish in appearance. Within a few hours, these colours frequently change in order to more effectively camouflage the egg upon its substrate. For example, the eggs of *Morpho peleides* are hemispherical, and their green colouration serves to conceal them extremely effectively on the upper surfaces of the leaves upon which they are laid.

The location in which the egg of a butterfly is deposited varies widely from species to species. Some butterflies lay their eggs within tiny cracks of bark, while others prefer the forks of twigs, the leaves of the hostplant, and sometimes foliage which is in close proximity to the hostplant itself. In the latter case, the newborn larva must undertake a journey from where it hatches, in order to locate its correct foodplant.

Eggs may be deposited in a variety of different manners. Some species of butterflies lay their eggs singly upon their hostplants, while others deposit them in clusters of variable sizes. Usually, these preferences are linked to the eventual habits of the future larvae. Some larvae are sedentary, while others may be gregarious, and in the latter case may complete their growth synchronously upon the same plant.

Many plants, such as Passion flower vines (*Passiflora* species), have evolved physical structures such as yellow nodes on their stems, which seem to serve the purpose of mimicking the eggs of *Heliconius* butterflies. Many *Passifloras* also possess yellow spots upon their leaves, which appear to serve the same purpose. These features have apparently developed in order to discourage females of *Heliconius* species from ovipositing upon the plants in question. The butterflies appear to prefer to deposit their eggs upon vines which do not already bear ova of other butterflies. Eggs which already exist upon such plants will produce larvae that will be more advanced in development in comparison to those which would be the result of more recent arrivals. Consequently, such further progressed larvae will possess much better chances for their eventual survival. It is therefore of benefit for the females to search for vines which are totally unutilized. Competition for survival is fierce, even at this early juncture in the development of butterflies.

Usually, the eggs of most butterflies require several days in order for the larvae to develop and hatch, but there are some exceptions to this rule. The eggs of *Morpho* butterflies may take up to twelve days, as do those of *Caligo* species (Brassolinae).

In many instances, the eggs of butterflies change in colour during their development. The eggshells of some species may take on a glassy appearance shortly before the larvae are due to hatch. The brown heads and pink and white body colouration of developing Owl Butterfly larvae may be clearly observed through their egg shells shortly before they emerge from them.

There are dangers present which jeopardize the development of a butterfly even before the larva hatches. Tiny wasps, such as those of the family Trichogrammatidae frequently deposit their own eggs inside those of many butterflies. The larvae of these wasps then proceed to complete their growth by feeding upon the contents of the butterfly egg in which they were laid. Eventually, the adult wasps hatch inside of the empty eggshell, and chew tiny holes through it in order to escape and breed. A dozen or more of these minute wasps may emerge from a single butterfly egg, which attests as to how minuscule these parasites are.

In tropical regions such as Costa Rica, many eggs of butterflies are killed by a variety of fungi and molds, which occur abundantly within the humid environments of tropical forests. Eggs which are deposited upon smaller hostplants may also be consumed by larvae which may already be in development upon the plants in question.

Ants also take a toll of butterfly eggs, because many species of ants are involved in complex symbiotic relationships with the same plants that butterflies utilize as larval hosts. Many varieties of Passion flower vines provide ants with sugary secretions, which they secrete from nodes situated upon their stems called extra-floral nectaries. Ants have a vested interest in guarding such sources of nutrition, for example from the attention of *Heliconius* butterflies, the larvae of which consume the leaves of these plants.

Although *Heliconius* larvae do not drink from extra-floral nectaries, they often defoliate the plants that they feed upon. This may result in the death of the plant in question, and the resultant destruction of the ant's food source. As a result, ants will usually dispose of the eggs of these butterflies, and their larvae, whenever they encounter them.

Consequently, butterflies must often practice a variety of adaptive behaviours in order to effectively co-exist upon the same plants that ants inhabit. *Heliconius* butterflies and other genera of the same subfamily (Heliconiinae) usually deposit their eggs upon the extremities of *Passiflora* plants, such as the tips of tendrils, or upon developing leaf shoots. These are locations where ants rarely choose to venture, and as a result, the eggs are less likely to be discovered and disposed of.

The Larva

The larva (or caterpillar), is the second stage in the development of a butterfly, and constitutes the phase of maximum growth (Fig. 1.3). Butterfly larvae are in reality little more than eating machines. They are comprised of a large gut, legs and powerful mandibles. The sole purpose of the larva is to feed and grow rapidly, which is a task that most are extremely efficient in performing.

Fig 1.3   The basic structures of a butterfly larva
(Papilio garamas).

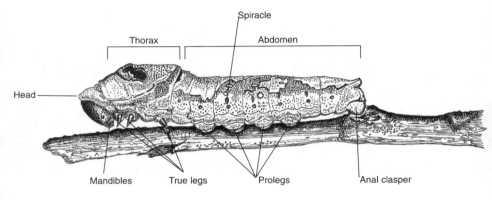

Before initiating its feeding phase, the young larva must first escape from its eggshell by creating an exit hole. Some larvae simply create a crude opening and squeeze through it, while others, such as those of *Caligo* species, snip a neat line around the top of the egg shell, which eventually opens in the manner of a lid.

As an initial meal, the hatchling will usually consume part, or all, of the its empty eggshell before commencing to feed upon foliage. This provides the young larva with valuable sustenance, should it have to search for a suitable plant to feed upon.

The larva of a butterfly is composed of thirteen flexible body segments and a head (Fig. 1.3). The latter structure possesses simple eyes, silk-spinning organs, and the powerful mandibles which enable the larva to consume large amounts of foliage rapidly (Fig. 1.4).

Fig 1.4   The head capsule of a butterfly larva *(Caligo atreus)*, illustrating its basic structures.

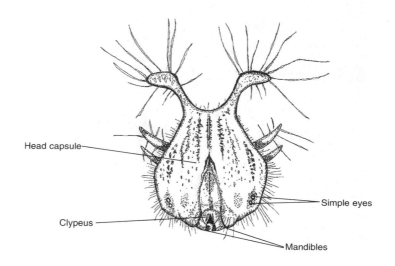

Head capsule

Clypeus

Simple eyes

Mandibles

The first three body segments behind the head of the larva bear a pair of legs beneath each, which are referred to as "true-legs" (Fig. 1.3). These "true-legs" will in due time become the legs of the adult butterfly. There are also pairs of flexible "prolegs" (Fig. 1.3), located beneath each of segments six through nine, which provide the larva with locomotion. Visible upon the terminal body segment of the caterpillar is a pair of specialized prolegs which are commonly referred to as "claspers" (Fig. 1.3). The claspers are utilized by the larva in order to securely grip its hostplant.

Situated upon each side of the first eight segments of the larva's body are minute openings which are referred to as spiracles (Fig. 1.3), through which respiration takes place.

A few days after the larva begins to feed, it has grown as much as is possible within its present skin. Its skin must now be replaced with a newer and more elastic one in order for it to continue development. The process of shedding the skin is called ecdysis, and occurs after the larva ceases to feed, and rests for approximately thirty-six to forty-eight hours. Prior to ecdysis, a silken mat is spun by the caterpillar, to which it anchors itself securely by its prolegs.

When the appropriate time arrives, the skin behind the head of the larva splits, usually along a dorsal suture, and the creature literally "walks out" of its old skin. After a few hours of resting, during which the feeding structures become rigid, the larva commences to feed once again. Each stage of larval growth is referred to as an instar, of which there are usually five in most species of butterflies.

As it grows, the morphology (or appearance) of butterfly larvae may change from instar to instar. The larvae of most Swallowtail butterflies (Papilionidae) begin their development as excellent imitations of fresh bird droppings, being brown and white in colouration, and extremely shiny in appearance. When these larvae mature, they often assume green colourations, and may possess markings upon their thoracic areas which closely resemble the eyes of snakes.

Larvae are very prone to being attacked by a variety of predators during their development. Parasitic flies of the family Tachinidae (Fig. 1.5), and wasps of families such as the Braconidae and Ichneumonidae (Fig. 1.5), take a heavy toll of the caterpillars of butterflies, in order to facilitate the development of their own larvae.

Fig 1.5   Some common parasites of butterfly larvae and pupae. A: An Ichneumon wasp (Ichneumonidae); B: A Tachnid fly (Tachinidae); C: An Apanteles wasp (Braconidae).

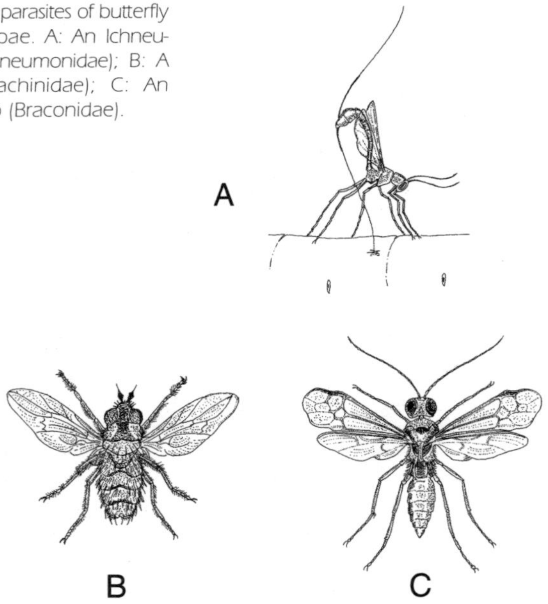

Tachinid flies frequently deposit their eggs directly upon the leaves of the foodplants that butterfly larvae consume, which are then eaten together with the leaf tissues as the caterpillars feed. The fly larvae quickly hatch inside the bodies of the caterpillars in question, and commence to feed upon the living tissues of the affected larvae. When their development is complete, the Tachinid larvae burrow directly through the skins of their dead or dying hosts in order to complete their metamorphoses.

Wasps of the family Ichneumonidae usually lay a single egg inside a larva or pre-pupa, which then supplies the solitary larva of the wasp with an ample food supply. The wasp genus **Apanteles** (Braconidae) usually deposit large numbers of eggs inside their larval or pupal hosts. **Apanteles** larvae utilize an ingenious method of keeping their hosts alive for long enough to complete their own feeding spans. Initially, their larvae attack the fatty tissues of their hosts, which enables the affected butterfly larvae to survive relatively unscathed while the wasp larvae slowly gain size. The vital tissues and organs of the caterpillars are then consumed last, after which the wasp larvae are fully grown, and emerge to spin their cocoons and pupate upon the remains of their hosts.

Concealment is a strategy which is used by the majority of butterfly larvae in order to escape the attentions of a variety of predators. This strategy may involve very effective types of camouflage, which are often used in conjunction with adaptive behaviours such as limiting feeding activity to times when light conditions are low, or becoming active only under the cover of darkness. Many predators are therefore far less able to find the larvae purely by visual means, as in the case of birds and small mammals.

Young larvae of **Catonephele** butterflies (Nymphalinae) commence feeding upon the leaf tips of their **Alchornea** foodplants (Euphorbiaceae). The leaf tissue is gradually eaten away from each side of the midrib, which results in the creation of a dry brown appendage. It is upon this dry section of midrib that the larvae rest when they are not feeding, which serves to effectively conceal them from predators.

The immature larvae of **Caligo** species often gather in large congregations along the mid-ribs of the banana leaves upon which they feed. These larvae develop patches of brown markings on their dorsal surfaces, which are extremely similar in nature to the leaf damage which is characteristic of banana plants. This patterning disrupts the shape of these larvae extremely well, and even a trained observer may easily pass them over while searching for them.

As they reach maturity, **Caligo** larvae may exceed 12 centimeters or more in length. At this juncture, their usual habit is to rest upon the brown and dry growth of the trunk of the banana tree. By following a feeding cycle that is usually timed to the hours of dawn and dusk, the larvae crawl up from their resting places to feed, and subsequently return to them in order to slowly digest their meals. The olive green or brown colouration of these larvae, and their fine, fuzzy texture, serves to blend them most effectively into the background upon which they are resting, thus providing excellent camouflage. The mature larvae of **Morpho** species also adopt a similar timetable with regard to their feeding behaviour. Such habits also serve to provide the observer with a very convenient and predictable method of monitoring the habits of certain types of caterpillars.

Another means by which butterfly larvae avoid predation is by consuming toxic species of plants. Such caterpillars usually advertize the fact that they taste very badly as a result of this strategy by utilizing bright colourations, which serve to ATTRACT the attention of would-be predators.

The larvae of many species of **Parides** Swallowtail butterflies (Papilionidae) are coloured in deep purple, white and yellow, which makes them very conspicuous upon the poisonous **Aristolochia** vines that they consume. Although a certain proportion of these larvae may be sampled as prospective meals, a predator which does so is unlikely to repeat the exercise after tasting a bitter mouthful of caterpillar. Such predators soon make a connection between the appearance of such larvae and the resultant unpleasant experience that they have received, and will generally avoid consuming any larvae which possess similar visual characteristics.

An accessory to bright colouration is the utilization of stinging spines and irritating hairs, which serve to discourage predators from eating the bristly owners of these features. The larvae of **Catonephele** and **Heliconius** species possess long and often sharp spines, which may cause irritations upon sensitive skins, and worse consequences in the mouths and throats of birds or other predators. Even the well camouflaged larvae of **Morpho** butterflies possess bristles and tufts of hairs, which clothe their heads and bodies. The latter features will readily break off into skin if these larvae are molested, and cause severe itching and rashes in the experience of the author.

The feeding span of larvae varies greatly from species to species, but generally speaking, three to four weeks would be the norm that most would require to complete their development. Extremes run from approximately twelve days for full larval maturation in certain *Heliconius* species, to eight weeks or more in the case of *Morpho* and *Caligo* butterflies.

Upon finishing its feeding phase, the larva now enters a stage which is referred to as the pre-pupa. At this juncture, the caterpillar usually voids its gut of remaining food, and may frequently engage in a wandering phase. The latter activity may involve leaving the hostplant entirely, in order to locate a suitable site for the purposes of pupation. There may be a very practical reason for this behaviour. Feeding damage that is evident upon the leaves of a hostplant may provide a visual cue to predators that there may be larvae feeding upon it. By abandoning the plant altogether, the pre-pupal larva may bring less attention to itself during the time spent in an immobile and vulnerable state while preparing for the process of pupation. Swallowtail butterflies generally follow this rule, as do many species of the family Nymphalidae. However, the larvae of *Morpho* butterflies are usually content to pupate wherever they happen to finish feeding. These larvae gradually lose their brown cryptic colouration at the conclusion of their final larval instar, and become green pre-pupae, which are extremely inconspicuous upon the hostplant. Certain other butterflies, such as *Heliconius sapho*, prefer to pupate gregariously, as do species of *Catasticta* butterflies (Pierinae).

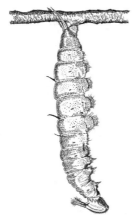

Fig 1.6   The pre-pupal larva of *Caligo eurilochus sulanus* (Brassolinae).

Fig 1.7   The pre-pupal larva of *Papilio polyxenes stabilis* (Papilioninae).

The Pupa

There are two usual positions that butterfly larvae assume in order to facilitate their transformations into pupae. These involve either hanging upside down freely by the tail (Fig. 1.6), or alternatively by being anchored by the terminal abdominal segment to a twig or other suitable support, with the head being held upright by a fine belt of silk which has been spun in order to provide support (Fig. 1.7). After attaching itself to its substrate, the pre-pupa rests while the pupa develops beneath the larval skin. This entire process usually requires thirty-six to forty-eight hours to complete.

At the appropriate juncture, the larval skin splits along a suture behind the larval head capsule. The skin is then gradually pulled along by a series of muscular contractions, which slowly reveals the soft skin of the pupa. Within a few minutes, the entire skin of the former larva has been pulled to the tail of the newly formed pupa, where it is cast off entirely. The pupa is now attached firmly to its silken support by the means of tiny hooks located upon the terminal abdominal segment, which are connected to a small structure called the cremaster.

A series of movements and contortions are now undertaken by the still soft pupa in order for it to assume its correct shape and posture. If this routine is not followed, the pupa may become deformed, and the structure of the future butterfly will not develop properly inside of it. This may result in a crippled butterfly, or the eventuality of the emerging insect not being able to free itself from the pupa when the time for hatching arrives.

The vast majority of Costa Rican butterflies form pupae which are excellently camouflaged. Different disguises include resemblances to chips of wood, leaf buds and shrivelled leaves. Some pupae, such as those of the large Nymphalid butterfly *Historis odius*, wriggle furiously when molested, which may serve to frighten and discourage curious would-be predators.

Catonephele numilia pupates upon the upper surfaces of leaves, with its pupa being positioned horizontally in relation to its support, instead of hanging freely by the tail as is the general rule for the family that this species belongs to.

The immobile state of the pupal stage makes pupae extremely vulnerable to attack. In particular, parasitic wasps and flies are now presented with an ideal opportunity to deposit their eggs at their leisure through the soft skins of newly formed pupae. These pupae will eventually become living banquets for the larvae of these parasites.

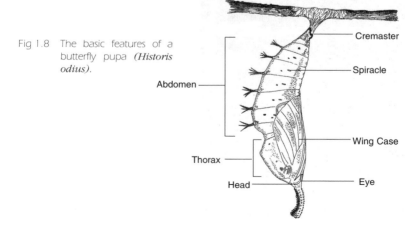

Fig 1.8 The basic features of a butterfly pupa *(Historis odius)*.

Cremaster

Spiracle

Abdomen

Wing Case

Thorax

Head

Eye

Visible upon the pupa are the structures of the future butterfly, such as its wings, legs, eyes and body sections (Fig. 1.8). Inside the pupa, changes are taking place which will gradually serve to complete the process of metamorphosis. Tissues are broken down, and dormant clusters of cells multiply in order to construct the butterfly. This process may take as little as two weeks, or a month or more, depending upon the species in question.

A relevant factor which frequently influences the period of pupal development is the weather. In seasonally dry areas of Costa Rica, such as province of Guanacaste, the appearance of many butterflies is markedly seasonal, as a result of protracted dry conditions. In seasonally dry zones, the foodplants that are necessary for larval development may be deciduous in nature, which does not allow certain butterflies to reproduce constantly. In such situations, the pupae of many species may lie dormant for several months until favourable weather appears once again. The development of such butterflies is eventually triggered by the arrival of seasonal rains. Such rains also serve to effectively synchronize the emergence of the insects, providing them with more guaranteed access to mates, food sources, and suitable larval hostplants. After the rains fall, there is usually a rapid profusion of plant growth, which permits their larvae to develop upon lush new foliage.

The Emergence of the Adult

The emergence of a butterfly from the pupa is truly one of nature's miracles. Generally speaking, the pupa will darken or change somewhat in appearance before the butterfly hatches. In many cases, the wing colours that the insect will possess are clearly visible through the pupal skin when emergence is imminent.

When the time for hatching (or eclosion) arrives, the skin of the pupa fractures where the head and legs are positioned, and the butterfly slowly pushes this section of the pupa open with its legs. Carefully, the insect extracts itself from the pupal shell, freeing itself of its confinement (Fig. 1.9). Immediately after emergence, the butterfly appears at first to be all legs and body. Wastes which have accumulated during the pupal phase are now expelled in the form of a brown or red liquid called meconium.

A butterfly's wings initially resemble tiny, soft, pads of colour, but soon start to increase in size as a result of the insect forcing blood into them from its bloated abdomen (Fig. 1.10). A network of veins within each of the wings starts to extend under the pressure of the blood circulating through them (Fig. 1.11), and within several minutes the wings expand to their maximum size (Fig. 1.12). The upper and lower wing membranes are fused together during this process, and gradually harden in contact with the air to provide the rigid structures that will permit the butterfly to take flight. Patternings upon the wings are now fully visible, and the insect is in its most perfect state.

While its wings are still soft at this critical juncture, the butterfly is extremely vulnerable to attacks made by birds, lizards, spiders and other predators. The drying process may last for one or two hours, during which time the butterfly carefully flexes and tests its wing muscles, in order to strengthen and prepare them for flight. Most butterflies seem to emerge in the early hours of the morning, which in the context of timing would seem to provide them with better visual concealment from predators whilst this delicate process is completed fully.

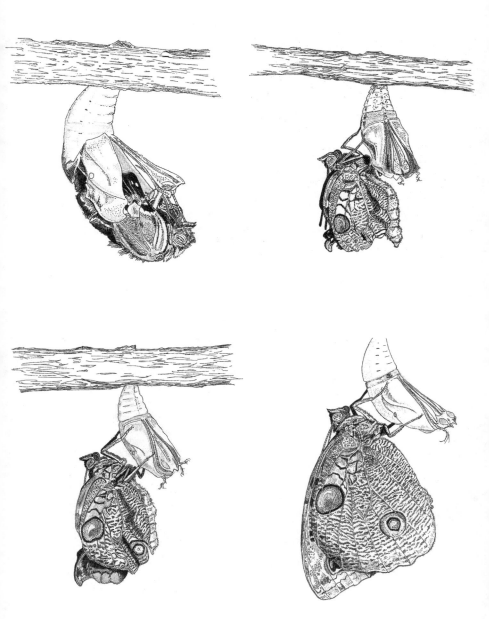

Fig 1.9 - 1.12   The emergence and wing expansion
of *Opsiphanes cassina fabricii*
(Brassolinae).

What Do Butterflies Eat?

In temperate regions of the world, the most readily identifiable food source that butterflies utilize is nectar, which is gathered by the insects from flowers. However, in tropical regions such as Costa Rica, the competition for nectar is much greater than in temperate zones of the world. This is because this resource is also utilized by hummingbirds, bats, as well as a multitude of other insects. Therefore, many of the butterflies which inhabit Costa Rica have adapted in order to utilize a variety of alternate food sources in order to survive.

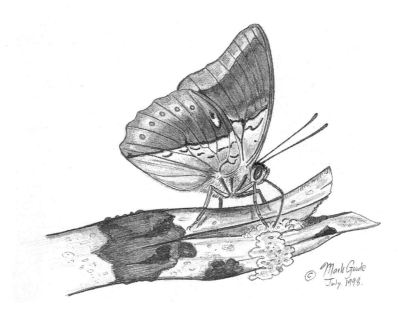

Fig 1.13   The butterfly *Prepona omphale* (Charaxinae) feeding upon a fermenting banana.

Fermenting Fruits

One of the most popular alternatives to nectar are the juices of rotting or fermenting fruits, of which there is an enormous variety available. Fruits which are particularly attractive to Costa Rican butterflies include bananas, mangos, papayas and those from a variety of species of palms. If one inspects the ground under a tree where any of the above fruits have fallen, a great variety of butterflies may often be discovered while feasting upon the fermenting juices that ooze from them (Fig. 1.13). In such situations, the butterflies frequently become intoxicated, and as a result are more readily approachable than would normally be the case.

Tree Sap

Another source of nourishment that is widely utilized by many Costa Rican butterflies is tree sap. The author has witnessed individual butterflies returning over periods of several consecutive days in order to utilize this resource. Many varieties of Cracker butterflies (*Hamadryas* species) are regular visitors to such situations, as are *Morpho* and *Caligo* species.

Mammal Dung

Fresh mammal dung, especially that which is produced by carnivores, is also very attractive as a source of nourishment to many butterflies. In particular, members of the subfamily Charaxinae, such as *Archaeoprepona* species, respond rapidly to dung if it is utilized as a lure. *Archaeoprepona* butterflies will make several exploratory flights around such baits before they eventually settle to feed. Each reconnaissance may often be punctuated with apparent observations which are made by the insect of the area surrounding the food source, usually from a perch upon a tree trunk or branch directly above the lure. One senses tangible "intelligence" on behalf of these butterflies while watching such apparent manifestations of sensitivity and nervousness. However, once they have settled and have commenced to feed, such butterflies may be approached with relative ease if one takes care to avoid any noises or sudden movements.

Nutritional Supplements

There are also types of nourishment that butterflies seem to need as a necessity for reproduction. A case in point is the subfamily Ithomiinae, of which many species are popularly referred to as "Glasswings". Females within this subfamily appear to require nitrogen in order to facilitate egg production. Nitrogen is gathered by these insects as a result of them feeding upon fresh bird droppings. The males of Ithomiine species apparently need to gather types of alkaloids in order to manufacture the pheromones necessary to stimulate courtship and mating. These alkaloids appear to be collected by the means of nectaring upon plants such as *Heliotropum* (Boraginaceae). The author has observed large assemblages of males representing many different Ithomiine species, upon the latter plants in Costa Rica and many other countries in Latin America.

Heliconius butterflies are capable of extracting nutrients from flower pollen, as well as nectar, and are able to store this food source upon their proboscises. These so called "pollen loads" may be readily observed upon most *Heliconius* butterflies that one sees in nature, and are evident as a white or yellow mass which is usually situated near the base of the insect's proboscis. This feeding strategy enables these butterflies to gradually consume the accumulated pollen at their leisure. Adaptions such as this may assist in enabling such butterflies to weather times when pollen and nectar may be scarce, or periods of sustained wet or cool conditions which would not serve to facilitate their usual feeding routines. *Heliconius* butterflies also utilize pollen for egg production, as well as to manufacture their chemical defenses.

Flower Nectar

Of course, many butterflies are able to survive on a simple diet of flower nectar. Popular nectar sources for Costa Rican butterflies include the blooms of Lantana, Hibiscus, Milkweeds *(Asclepias)*, Bougainvillea, Zinnias and Verbena *(Stachytarpheta)*.

It may be discovered through simple observation that certain species or genera are attracted to flowers of particular types or colours. For example, the yellow and orange *Phoebis* butterflies (Coliadinae) are strongly drawn to red coloured nectar sources, and may be frequently encountered while nectaring upon the red blossoms of Hibiscus and Bougainvillea.

CHAPTER II

MIMICRY AND SEXUAL DIMORPHISM IN BUTTERFLIES

Mimicry

When the butterflies of Costa Rica are observed in nature, one often notices how many of these insects resemble each other to a great degree. Combinations of wing colourations that are frequently observed are black, yellow and orange, and also black, red and white. Such manifestations of conspicuous colouration are referred to as being aposematic in nature, that is, patterning which is intended to be registered as a warning to potential predators. Such warnings are based upon the fact that many of the owners of such livery are toxic, and quite inedible to most predators.

Upon closer inspection, it will become apparent to the observer that many of these similar looking butterflies are very alike in colouration, but often very different in size and details of their structure. This is because a great many species of Costa Rican butterflies have evolved very similar appearances to each another, guises which are referred to as mimicry (Plate 1). The purpose of mimicry is for edible species of butterflies to closely resemble different related, or non-related varieties which are protected by toxic chemical compounds that are stored within their body tissues. These so called "mimics" are endowed with a presumed degree of protection from the effects of predation, as a result of resembling distasteful species of butterflies which may be relatively immune to being eaten.

Within the Costa Rican context, an explanation as to the workings of mimicry may be made upon the premise of a bird such as a Jacamar (Galbulidae) attacking a noxious and bad tasting butterfly, such as a female of **Parides arcas** (Papilionidae). The bird captures the butterfly, removes its wings and proceeds to swallow it. Shortly afterwards, it vomits up the remains of the insect and wipes the foul tasting residues upon the branch it is perching on. This ghastly experience will discourage this bird from attacking any species of butterfly that even remotely resembles the black, red and white **MODEL** species it had attempted to consume. Consequently, when the bird observes an example of **Papilio anchisiades** (Papilionidae), which is a very similar butterfly that belongs to the same family as **Parides arcas**, it will most likely pass it over as a prospective meal, even though this **MIMIC** may be quite edible. It is therefore of the greatest benefit to the mimic to resemble its model as closely as possible.

In nature, the usual rule that mimics follow is to be less common than their models. For example, **Heliconius hecale** is an abundant model species of lowland rainforest habitats, where its far less common mimic, **Consul fabius** (Charaxinae) also occurs. If this mimic were as abundant as its model, more of the former would be available to sample as a possible first and palatable meal. As a result, many predators might not have as of yet associated the model with an unpleasant experience, so more of the mimics might be consumed as a result; a factor which would obviously not run in their favour.

There are two main types of so-called "protective mimicry", which clearly demonstrate convergences in patterning and colouration. These are known respectively as Batesian and Mullerian Mimicry (Plate 1).

Batesian Mimicry

This theory of mimicry was formulated by H.W. Bates, a naturalist and collector of butterflies who made numerous discoveries of these insects while exploring the Amazon during the nineteenth century.

His assertion was that many species of palatable butterflies have evolved colourations and patternings which are extremely similar to many species that are unpalatable. Therefore there exist less common edible mimic species and more numerous inedible models. The implied result of this theory is that the mimics gain a degree of protection from predation due to having evolved a very similar appearance to that of their models.

Mullerian Mimicry

Mullerian mimicry is a concept put forward by the naturalist Fritz Muller, also during the nineteenth century. His theory states that a variety of inedible species of butterflies mimic each other in order to gain a degree of mutual protection from predation.

A possible advantage to be gained with regard to this sort of mimicry is that these different toxic species may exist at relatively high and even population levels. This is because these butterflies are presumably all quite distasteful, and no obligation exists on the part of one or the other to be sacrificed and sampled as the "first meal".

Crypsis

Crypsis, a term which is more popularly referred to as camouflage, manifests itself as a type of mimicry which involves the utilization of colourations or patternings that assist in enabling an organism to conceal itself effectively from potential predators. Many Costa Rican butterflies have evolved excellent forms of crypsis, in particular the many species which feed primarily on rotting fruits and other food sources upon the forest floor.

A very popular method of crypsis involves wing patterning and colouration which closely resembles that of dried leaves or tree bark. This is an extremely efficient means of concealment for butterflies which commonly feed amidst the leaf litter within forests. Such a guise may enable a butterfly to feed on its food source in a manner of relative security.

Butterflies of the genus *Memphis* (Charaxinae) are excellent mimics of dried leaves, and one can almost step upon them while they are feeding before they are detected, and subsequently fly away with great vigor in order to escape capture.

It would seem to generally be the case that butterflies which utilize crypsis are quite edible to a variety of predators. As a result, effective camouflage may be crucial in order for such butterflies to survive, as many are not seemingly included in mimicry complexes, and appear not to have developed distasteful properties.

Disruptive Colouration

Many species of butterflies have evolved forms of disruptive patterning and colouration. These qualities serve to break up and blur the shape of the insects while they are at rest. *Morpho* butterflies often possess large "eyespots", called ocelli, as components of their wing markings (Fig. 2.1). These features are usually positioned near the edges of the undersides of their wings. This patterning is two-fold in purpose, being both an excellent disruptive pattern, and also an effective focal point in situations when predators attempt to attack them. The wing ocelli are similar in function to that of bullseyes, and appear to serve as a means of concentrating attacks upon less vulnerable areas of these butterflies, other than the bodies of the insects themselves.

Fig 2.1   The undersurfaces of the wings of *Morpho peleides limpida* (Morphinae), illustrating the large and conspicuous occelli present upon them.

Upon several occasions, the author has observed predators such as lizards attacking *Morpho* butterflies, and gripping them by their wings in the locations of their ocelli. Upon being attacked, the sections of the wings in question were seen to tear away, which allowed the insects an opportunity to escape.

Many examples of butterflies that possess wing occelli within their patterning will often be observed in nature to have these features damaged, or missing, as a result of attempted predation. The simple fact that these insects survived such attacks demonstrates that they are a living testament to the effectiveness of this strategy as a form of defense against mortality in nature.

Caligo species are frequently observed in nature to have portions of the large occelli on their hindwings removed. In many cases, identical sections of each of the hindwings are missing on both wings. This would strongly suggest that these features are of great value with regard to *Caligo* species, in order for them to successfully survive attempts at predation.

Sexual Dimorphism

Many of Costa Rica's butterflies exhibit differences in colouration, patterning, size and shape, with regard to the different sexes of the species in question. This is referred to as sexual dimorphism (Plate 6). Species of butterflies which exhibit this characteristic are frequently involved as members of mimicry complexes, and may be either edible or inedible.

Within any specific genus of butterflies, similar colourations may be shared, especially if they are species of a toxic nature. The females of *Parides* butterflies that occur in Costa Rica frequently share the same habitats, and are coloured in the same scheme of red, black and white. Indeed, *Parides* are very difficult to separate as to the species in question, even by trained observers who study specimens in museums.

It is obviously of mutual benefit for species such as *Parides* butterflies to share similar physical appearances when they happen to co-exist in the same habitats. As a result, less examples of each butterfly will be required to be sampled as prey than would be the case if they exhibited more divergent forms of colouration and patterning.

Morpho butterflies are also excellent examples of sexual dimorphism. Many of the metallic blue species, such as *Morpho cypris* and *Morpho amathonte*, exhibit females which are quite subdued in colouration in comparison to their male counterparts. Some *Morpho* females may lack metallic colouration totally, as is the case of the ochre coloured females of *Morpho cypris*.

The purpose of these differences in colouration would seem to be that they aid in drawing less attention to the females as they go about the important business of egg-laying. Indeed, the females of *Morpho amathonte*, which are usually observed in the shadier areas of their forest habitats, may be relatively inconspicuous while they are active, even taking in account that they are very large butterflies.

On the other hand, the metallic blue wings of many male *Morpho* butterflies appear to be utilized in behavioral interactions, which enable territories to be established. Upon many occasions, the author has witnessed males of *Morpho peleides* meet along the edges of forests, briefly make contact with each other, and subsequently fly away rapidly in opposite directions. This may indicate that the colourations of *Morpho* butterflies are utilized in order for individuals of the same species to identify each other, and serve the purpose of helping to maintain the boundaries of territories that the individual insects have established.

Sexual dimorphism would seem to be an important factor with regard to natural selection in many species of butterflies that occur in Costa Rica. Although the males of certain butterflies may fall victim more readily to predators as the result of not closely resembling toxic models, the utilization of mimicry, or forms of less conspicuous patterning by the females of such species may greatly improve their chances of achieving greater longevity in nature.

CHAPTER III

THE CLASSIFICATION OF BUTTERFLIES

In order to classify any organism, it is necessary to use a framework known as systematics. This provides a method by which scientists and others may rationalize as to how different organisms are related to each other. It also permits a framework to be constructed by which the evolution of organisms may be charted out in as accurate a manner as possible.

The originator of the binomial system which is utilized in systematics was the Swede Carolus Linnaeus (1707-1778). In essence, the binomial system consists of both a genus and species name in order to identify all organisms. The function of this system is similar to that of a surname and given name, which a variety of human societies also utilize.

Linnaeus created this system of classification based upon different categories of distinctiveness. However, since this system was created, our knowledge of the animal kingdom has increased to the point where additional categories are currently required in order to more accurately classify an organism. Currently, a butterfly is usually classified as to its given **family, subfamily, genus, species** and **subspecies.**

The organization of butterflies into **families** allows species of similar structure and characteristics to be grouped together and studied independently of other species which do not share the same distinctive features. Within different families of butterflies there are further groupings called **subfamilies**. Subfamilies are used to organize species which belong to the same family, but which are considered as being distinctive enough collectively to be identified as separable from the greater whole.

Subfamilies share the same basic physical structures as the family to which they belong, but they may exhibit consistent differences with regard to certain characters, often within several different genera. An excellent example would be the subfamily Brassolinae, which is represented by the Owl Butterflies (*Caligo* species), and other genera such as *Opsiphanes* and *Eryphanis*. Although these genera are not identical in appearance, there are visible characters which are common to all of them. These include well developed occelli on the undersides of their wings, and androconial structures in the males that are extremely similar in design. The larvae of the different genera within the Brassolinae also show many close affinities to each other, which lends further credence to the overall distinctiveness of the Brassolinae within the greater family Nymphalidae.

A **genus** name is applied to a group of butterflies which share close similarities with regard to their physical structures, appearance and colouration. For example, *Caligo atreus* refers to a butterfly within the genus *Caligo*, and the given species name of *atreus*. It resembles its relative *Caligo eurilochus* in that it has a similar shape to its wings, and possesses well developed occelli upon its hindwings (Fig. 3.1). However, it diverges with regard to details of its size, wing patterning, and coloration from the latter species. This justifies its designation of being a closely related, but distinctive species in its own right, within the same genus.

Fig 3.1   Two butterflies which share the same genus.
A: *Caligo eurilochus sulanus*; B: *Caligo atreus dionysos*.

The **species** names which are created for use in this system are usually derived from latin or greek. In the case of the latter language, many species are named after Greek gods and goddesses. Most Morpho species are named after these personalities, such as *Morpho peleides*, *Morpho achilles*, and *Morpho polyphemus*, among others. However, new species of butterflies and other organisms are frequently given species names which refer to an individual who might have been involved in their discovery, or who may be perceived of being worthy of immortalization in this manner as a form of homage.

The next category is that of a **subspecies**. This refers to a distinctive geographical variety of a particular species which differs consistently in appearance from other populations within the distribution of the species in question.

For example, in Costa Rica, there exist two subspecies of *Morpho peleides*, namely *Morpho peleides marinita*, and *Morpho peleides limpida*. The former subspecies is brown with reduced areas of blue on the uppersides of its wings, while the latter one is black with wider expanses of blue colouration. Therefore, the use of a subspecies name more accurately identifies two consistently different individual populations of *Morpho peleides*.

Although an individual who is starting to learn about butterflies may find such naming slightly confusing or difficult, it is well worth the effort it takes to familiarize oneself with latin names. This is because the use of such names is a convenient way by which any one species of butterfly can be accurately identified throughout the world by individuals of any culture. Each country within the distribution of a certain species of butterfly may utilize a different "popular" name in a variety of different languages, which is obviously of little value to those who do not share the same tongue. Therefore, a Costa Rican butterfly farmer refers to *Morpho peleides* by the same name as the author does, and we both have exactly the same species in mind if a discussion about that particular butterfly ensues.

Butterfly Families Which Occur in Costa Rica

The butterfly families and subfamilies that are dealt with in this book are represented by species which may be readily observed by the visitor or resident. Purposefully excluded are families which contain varieties that are unlikely to be encountered, or which may be erratic in appearance. Therefore, the author has declined to include the families Lycaenidae and Riodinidae for the purposes of this work.

Consequently, the families and subfamilies that are presented to the reader include the following;

Family: **NYMPHALIDAE**

Subfamilies: BRASSOLINAE
CHARAXINAE
DANAINAE
HELICONIINAE
ITHOMIINAE
MORPHINAE
NYMPHALINAE
SATYRINAE

Family: **PAPILIONIDAE**

Subfamily: PAPILIONINAE
Tribe: LEPTOCERCINI
PAPILIONINI
TROIDINI

Family: **PIERIDAE**

Subfamilies: COLIADINAE
DISMORPHIINAE
PIERINAE

Family NYMPHALIDAE

Representatives of this diverse family of butterflies are distributed throughout the world. There are many divisions of subfamilies which are made within the Nymphalidae, with several of these occurring in Costa Rica. The feature which is most characteristic of Nymphalid butterflies relates to the structure of their first pair of legs. These legs are very reduced in size and stumpy in appearance, which leaves only two pairs of legs fully functional for walking.

Costa Rican representatives of the Nymphalidae occur throughout the country, in virtually all habitat types, and at all altitudes. The larvae of this family feed upon an enormous variety of hostplants, depending upon the subfamily, genus and

23

species in question. They are also equally diverse with regard to their physical appearances and habits.

The majority of Nymphalids feed upon a variety of food sources other than nectar as adults. Such nourishment may include mammal dung, juices from fermenting fruits, and also tree sap, which are good details to be aware of when one searches for these butterflies.

Subfamily BRASSOLINAE

Members of this subfamily are found throughout much of Latin America. A variety of different Brassoline genera occur in Costa Rica, such as *Caligo*, *Eryphanis*, *Opsiphanes*, *Dynastor* and *Catoblepia*. The large wing ocelli that species of the genus *Caligo* have evolved, have created the popular reference to these insects as being "Owl Butterflies". Species of Costa Rican Brassolinae are found most abundantly in rainforest habitats, but some species, such as *Opsiphanes cassina*, may be quite common even in urban areas.

These butterflies are active primarily during dawn and dusk, and often fly into lighted buildings at night. They are strongly attracted to rotting fruits and tree sap as food sources. By placing fermenting bananas along a trail in a forest, one will often discover several Brassoline species that have responded to these baits. Many species will also feed upon animal droppings.

One of the most notable characteristics of these butterflies are the well developed occelli that are included in the wing patterning of most species. These serve a similar function as those of *Morpho* butterflies, serving to concentrate the effects of attempted predation upon less vital areas of the insects. Many examples of the genus *Caligo* observed in nature will be seen to have the wing occelli partially intact or totally missing, testifying to their use for this purpose.

Fig 3.2   The stocky pupa of *Caligo memnon* (Brassolinae).

The larvae of Brassoline species feed upon a variety of foodplants such as Banana (Musaceae), Palms (Arecaceae) *Heliconia* species (Heliconiaceae), and Bamboos (Poaceae), and are typically adorned with configurations of spines, knobs and clubs upon their head capsules. The latter features vary greatly from species to species within the different genera, and serve as an excellent means by which to accurately identify different varieties of larvae.

Pupae of Brassolines hang by the tail, and are cryptically coloured in shades of brown, grey or green. Often there are small silver spots located upon the wing cases, which resemble drops of dew. The pupae of *Caligo* species are often huge and are covered in sparse short bristly hairs (Fig. 3.2).

Subfamily CHARAXINAE

Charaxines are common elements of the butterfly fauna in virtually all habitats and altitudes in Costa Rica, and are represented by a variety of diverse and often spectacular species. Genera of Costa Rican Charaxines which are commonly encountered include *Prepona, Archaeoprepona, Hypna and Memphis*.

Structurally, the bodies of these butterflies are compact and very powerfully muscled, which provides the insects with incredibly swift powers of flight. As adults, these butterflies feed almost exclusively upon decaying matter, such as fermenting fruits and dung.

Many species of this subfamily are observed relatively infrequently. This may be partly due to the fact that Charaxines are often residents of the canopies of forests, and descend very rarely to ground level. It can be a fascinating experience to leave baits along forest trails in order to attract members of this subfamily, and quietly wait to see which species appear. The response to baits is often very rapid, with some species often appearing after only several minutes of time have elapsed.

The eggs of Charaxines are usually globular in shape, and are generally deposited one to a leaf, although several may be laid upon the same plant by the same female. The larvae are usually smooth skinned, and are often well endowed with horns and other adornments upon their head capsules. They feed solitarily upon their hostplants, which commonly include *Piper* (Piperaceae), *Persea* (Lauraceae), and *Inga* species (Mimosaceae), among others.

Subfamily DANAINAE

Danaines are found throughout much of the world, but occur in their greatest variety in tropical Asia. A relatively small number of species are found in the New World, but a well known inclusion in the Costa Rican fauna is the Monarch butterfly (*Danaus plexippus*) which is famous for the extensive yearly migrations that its North American populations participate in.

These insects are extremely tough as adults, and possess bodies that are very resilient to crushing and other forms of damage, such as peckings from birds that attempt to prey upon them.

The larval foodplants of Costa Rican Danaines include *Asclepias* species (Asclepiadacae), which are commonly referred to as Milkweeds, and *Ficus* (Moracaeae). Milkweeds apparently provide a source of chemical protection for the Danaine butterflies which utilize them as a means for larval development.

In Costa Rica, Danaines are represented by genera such as *Danaus, Lycorea*, and *Anetia*. They are encountered most commonly in disturbed habitats,

25

which are most suitable for the weedy hostplants to prosper in. In the Central Valley, populations of Danaines are present at most times of the year. One specialized species, **Anetia thirza**, is a resident of cloud forest habitats in Costa Rica, and belongs to a genus that is found exclusively in the New World.

The eggs of these butterflies are usually barrel shaped, and are deposited singly upon the upper or undersurfaces of the hostplant's leaves. Danaine larvae are smooth skinned, usually quite colourful, and may possess fleshy mobile tubercles in species such as the Monarch butterfly (Fig. 3.3). The pupae are very rounded, smooth, and coloured in shades of pale green in the case of the genus **Danaus**.

Fig 3.3   The conspicuous striped larva of the Monarch butterfly (*Danaus plexippus*).

Subfamily HELICONIINAE

This subfamily is present throughout Central and South America, and also occurs in the southern United States. The Heliconiinae includes some very familiar Costa Rican butterflies, and is represented by genera such as **Heliconius**, **Eueides**, **Dione**, **Agraulis** and **Philaethria**. These butterflies are popularly referred to as "Longwings", due to the elongated shape of the forewings of most species.

The Heliconiinae have developed a very close ecological relationship with the plant family Passifloraceae, which are commonly known as Passion flowers, or as Granadilla in Costa Rica. These plants grow as vines or shrubs, and are very diverse in flower colouration and leaf shape. It is assumed that these plants have been utilized as hostplants by members of the Heliconiinae for a considerable period of time, as they have evolved a wide array of features that are seemingly intended to discourage their use in this regard. Examples of such plant defenses include structures that appear to mimic the eggs of these butterflies, which may serve to discourage females from ovipositing on the plants in question. **Passiflora** species have also evolved a great variety of leaf shapes. This strategy may serve to confuse the visual search images that female butterflies often utilize when seeking their correct hostplants.

Heliconiines are long lived butterflies, which may survive for several months. These insects are often very faithful to their nectar sources, and may visit the same flowers continually for a considerable period of time. Individuals of many species in this subfamily accumulate pollen on their proboscises, which is stored and utilized when nectar resources are limited. The pollen is diluted with digestive enzymes that are regurgitated by the butterfly, and is then subsequently drawn up the proboscis and consumed.

Species of the Heliconiinae are involved in mimicry complexes, both as apparent models and co-mimics. There are similar patterns and colourations to be found in different species of this subfamily throughout their range, with these characters often varying on a regional basis.

Pairs of species that exhibit almost identical patterning exist in Costa Rica, such as *Heliconius cydno* and *sapho*, and *Heliconius erato* and *melpomene* (Plate 1). The latter species of each of the prior two pairs are much less common in nature than their partners, and appear to be more specialized ecologically.

For example, the larvae of the common *Heliconius cydno* are **generalists,** which are able to successfully complete their growth upon several different varieties of *Passiflora*. In comparison, the larvae of *Heliconius sapho* are **specialists**, which appear to be capable of utilizing only one species of *Passiflora* for the same purpose, namely the uncommon *Passiflora pittieri*.

Nocturnal roosting behaviour is common in many species of Heliconiines. These roosts may include individuals of like or different species of these butterflies, which congregate together, often in large numbers, in order to sleep at the same locations on a nightly basis.

Subfamily ITHOMIINAE

Ithomiine butterflies are characteristic of the tropical regions of the New World, and are represented by a great variety of genera and species in Costa Rica.

These insects are usually involved as models and co-mimics in mimicry complexes throughout their distribution. Many species are commonly patterned in yellow, orange and black. Such genera as *Tithorea, Melinaea* and *Mechanitis* occur in Costa Rica, that possess such colouration. Other varieties, such as representatives of the genera *Oleria, Greta* and *Ithomia* possess wings which are quite transparent, and are commonly referred to as "Glasswings".

The larvae of most Ithomiine species feed upon members of the Nightshade family (Solanaceae), which are well known as producers of a multitude of toxins. The butterflies oviposit upon the foodplants either singly, or in clusters of variable quantities. In the latter case, the larvae develop communally upon the hostplant.

Fig. 3.4   An Ithomiine butterfly nectaring upon flowers at the Monteverde Cloud Forest Reserve.

Ithomiine butterflies are typical residents of forest habitats of all types in Costa Rica (Fig. 3.4), but may also be encountered in open areas while searching for their hostplants. These butterflies often participate in seasonal migrations due to climatic changes, and may often be encountered outside of their more typical shaded forest surroundings in such circumstances.

The males of a variety of Ithomiine species congregate in groups called **leks** within their habitats in order to attract mates, which is a behaviour known as leking. Leks may be composed of different species of Ithomiines, which group together to emit higher concentrations of pheromones to attract females. The pheromones of different species seem to be quite alike in chemical composition, and as a result, a variety of females and males utilize the same locations for the purposes of courtship.

Subfamily MORPHINAE

The subfamily Morphinae usually occurs in forest habitats from Mexico to South America. Most of the species of this subfamily belong to the spectacular and popular genus *Morpho*. Other genera include the secretive and interesting *Antirrhea* and *Caerois* species. All of these genera fly in Costa Rica.

Members of the Morphinae are popularly known by the brilliant metallic colourations that are displayed by a variety of species which are included in the genus *Morpho*, a feature which serves to make these creatures popular and sought after by observers and collectors alike. The undersides of the wings of *Morpho* species are often adorned with large configurations of ocelli. Popularly termed as "eye spots", these features appear to serve as diversionary features, the function of which is to concentrate attacks upon these insects away from their more vulnerable bodies, and instead to the edges of their wings.

A variety of plant families are utilized as foodplants for the larvae of Morphine species, including members of the pea family (Fabaceae), palms (Arecaceae) and bamboos (Poaceae). The larvae are most unusual among butterflies in that they are quite hairy, but often very colourful, particularly during their earlier instars (Fig. 3.5).

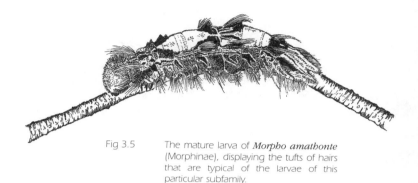

Fig 3.5   The mature larva of *Morpho amathonte* (Morphinae), displaying the tufts of hairs that are typical of the larvae of this particular subfamily.

When mature, *Morpho* caterpillars usually lose their bright colourations, and develop excellent cryptic patternings which makes them extremely difficult to detect while they rest upon the woody stems of their hostplants. The larvae of this subfamily usually exhibit a dawn and dusk feeding cycle, which serves to confine their activities to hours when they are less visible to potential predators.

Morpho butterflies feed exclusively upon decaying plant matter, such as rotting fruits and fermenting fungal growths. This is good to know if one wishes to utilize such food sources as baits, in order to observe the butterflies more closely. Once they commence feeding, *Morpho* butterflies are quite approachable if care is taken. Rotting bananas, palm fruits and mangos are particularly effective for such purposes.

Subfamily NYMPHALINAE

This subfamily contains a number of diverse genera. Among those that are dealt with in this book are *Historis, Nessaea, Hamadryas, Siproeta, Anartia* and *Catonephele*. Members of the Nymphalinae occur in all habitats, and at all elevations in Costa Rica. These butterflies feed upon a wide variety of food sources, including fermenting fruits and fungal growths, animal dung, urine and nectar.

Larvae of most of the species within the Nymphalinae possess variable adornments of spines, and usually feed as solitary individuals upon their hostplants. Many different foodplants are utilized by this subfamily for larval development, such as those of the plant families Euphorbiaceae, Acanthaceae, Sapindaceae, and Moraceae.

Nymphaline pupae are anchored to their chosen substrate by their tails. They may hang freely upside down, or in certain cases are positioned in a horizontal manner in relation to the upper surface of a leaf, such as in the genera *Catonephele* and *Nessaea* (Fig. 3.6). The pupae of this subfamily are often extremely cryptic, and consequently difficult to detect in nature.

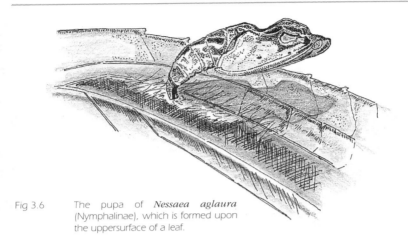

Fig 3.6   The pupa of ***Nessaea aglaura***
(Nymphalinae), which is formed upon
the uppersurface of a leaf.

Subfamily SATYRINAE

Species included within the subfamily Satyrinae are found at all elevations, and in all types of habitats in Costa Rica. The adults are characteristically plain in appearance and are usually coloured in shades of brown and grey, although some genera, such as ***Cithaerias***, possess transparent wings.

Most species of Satyrinae incorporate wing occelli into their patterning. The occelli of Satyrines seem to serve the same purpose of focusing predator attacks upon these features, as those evident in species within the subfamilies Morphinae and Brassolinae. Many individuals of different Satyrine genera will be observed in nature to have suffered wing damage that would attest to the effective function of these markings.

The majority of Satyrines feed upon grasses and bamboos (Poaceae) as larvae, but some genera, such as ***Pierella*** and ***Cithaerias***, utilize species of ***Heliconia*** (Heliconiaceae) for this purpose.

Satyrine larvae are usually solitary feeders, and frequently conceal themselves near the bases of their foodplants when not active, for example in the case of the genus ***Pierella***. The caterpillars of this subfamily are usually coloured in shades of green and brown, and are generally smooth skinned, although some may possess a swarthy skin texture. Pupae of this subfamily usually hang by the tail, but may sometimes be formed upon the ground within leaf litter.

The flight behaviour of these butterflies is generally slow, fluttering, and close to the ground. However ***Citheraeas*** and ***Pierella*** butterflies glide in a very controlled manner along the forest floor, and settle occasionally upon fallen leaves. Satyrines may perch in the sunlight at times, but are most often encountered in conditions of shade within forests, or along forest edges. Species which occur in open conditions generally become active when stimulated with sunlight, and their activities may be entirely absent without it.

Family PAPILIONIDAE

Butterflies of the family Papilionidae are sometimes referred to as "Swallowtails", and are distributed throughout much of the world. Included within this family are the huge Birdwing butterflies (***Ornithoptera***) of Indo-Australia, which are the largest butterflies in existence.

Subfamily PAPILIONINAE

The subfamily Papilioninae is divided into different groupings that are referred to as "tribes", of which three occur in Costa Rica. These divisions are based upon differences with regard to the structure of the butterflies, their early stages, and larval hostplants. In the balance of the New World, there are mimicry complexes which involve members of this family. The primary models are females of toxic ***Parides*** butterflies, which are also very similar co-mimics within their own genus.

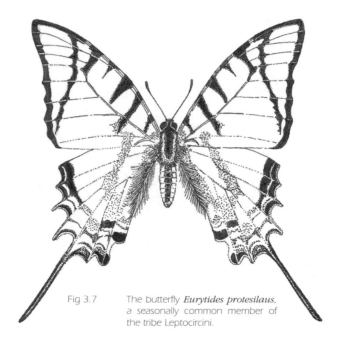

Fig 3.7   The butterfly ***Eurytides protesilaus***, a seasonally common member of the tribe Leptocircini.

Tribe LEPTOCIRCINI

A second tribe within the subfamily Papilioninae which occurs in Costa Rica, the Leptocircini, is represented by the genus ***Eurytides*** (Fig. 3.7). Many species within ***Eurytides*** are mimetic in relation to other Papilionid species and families of butterflies. The larvae of this genus feed mainly upon plants within the family Annonaceae, some of which produce fruits that are popularly referred to as "custard apples".

The adults of **Eurytides** may be tailed or tailless, and occur in a variety of habitats throughout Costa Rica. Some species are extremely seasonal in regard to their flight appearances, as is the case in Guanacaste province, which experiences long and pronounced dry periods. Shortly after the rains begin to fall, there are often large emergences of **Eurytides** in such areas. These butterflies may be frequently observed, sometimes by the hundreds, while drinking water from mud puddles.

Tribe PAPILIONINI

The tribe Papilionini includes the so-called "true swallowtails" of the genus **Papilio**, and is represented in Costa Rica by species such as **Papilio anchisiades**, **Papilio thoas**, and more unusual varieties such as **Papilio garamas**, which occurs only in high altitude cloud forest habitats.

These butterflies usually possess a tail-like projection on each hindwing, hence the popular name "swallowtail". **Papilios** are considered to be quite edible, and feed as larvae upon a wide variety of hostplants including **Citrus** (Rutaceae), Avocado (Lauraceae), **Piper** (Piperaceae) and members of the carrot family (Apiaciae).

Tribe TROIDINI

The genera **Battus** and **Parides** are included in a third tribe called the Troidini. This tribe includes most of the species which serve as the models for mimicry complexes involving other Costa Rican members of the Papilionidae, and also other non-related butterfly families.

Both of these genera feed as larvae upon vines of the family Aristolochiaceae. These plants are popularly known as "Pipevines" or "Dutchmans Pipes", in reference to the often large and pipe-shaped flowers that many species produce. Plants of this family manufacture toxins which are apparently utilized by these butterflies as a form of chemical defense. The odours that these insects produce as adults, and even pupae, can be quite strong, and may often be discernable even to the human nose.

Larvae of the genus **Battus** feed gregariously upon **Aristolochia** vines. In Costa Rica, **Battus** species are tailless as adults, and are usually coloured in black and bottle green, which makes them highly visible while they are active. The most familiar species of **Battus** that occurs in Costa Rica is **Battus polydamas**, which is commonly observed throughout the country.

Parides species are aposematically coloured in black, red and green in the case of males, and in females black, red and white. These butterflies lack well developed tails in Costa Rica, although species of **Parides** from other parts of Latin America may possess such features.

Parides larvae are solitary feeders, which are able to develop upon a variety of species of **Aristolochia** vines. The butterflies are usually residents of shaded forest habitats, and are very conspicuous while in flight. Common species of Costa Rican **Parides** butterflies include **Parides arcas** and **Parides iphidamas**.

The eggs of the Papilionidae are generally globular in shape, and may be deposited singly, or in clusters, depending upon the habits of the species in question.

Larvae of this family are very variable in appearance, but most mimic bird droppings in their early instars, being brown, white and very shiny. The mature larvae may be purple, brown or green in ground colouration. Depending upon the genus and species in question, the caterpillars are smooth skinned, or sometimes possess long, fleshy projections which are referred to as tubercles.

A structural feature that larvae of the Papilionidae possess is an extendable forked organ called an osmaterium. This structure is everted from behind the head of the caterpillar when it is disturbed, with a noxious bitter-sweet odour being released in the process. The true function of this organ is not well understood, but it may have value as a means of alarming potential predators when the larvae are annoyed.

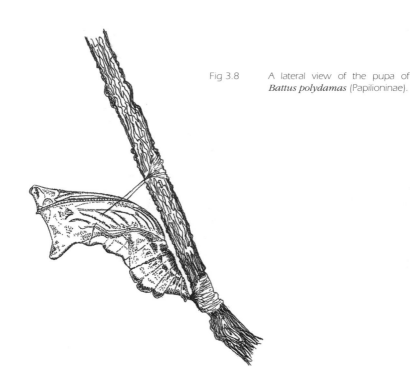

Fig 3.8   A lateral view of the pupa of *Battus polydamas* (Papilioninae).

Pupae of the Papilionidae are well camouflaged, and most are coloured in shades of brown. There are often projections present on the thoracic area of these pupae which resemble thorns or wood chips. Usually, the pupae are formed away from the larval hostplants, and are supported vertically by the means of a silken girdle, which is positioned around the body of the pupa (Fig. 3.8).

In Costa Rica, these butterflies occur in a variety of habitats. Depending upon the species in question, these environments range from sunny open areas, forest edges, and the canopies of forests. In the latter case, the insects descend to the ground upon brief occasions in order to oviposit or feed.

The males of many species of Papilionidae drink water from moistened earth shortly after they emerge from the pupa. This behaviour is not well understood, but it is assumed that the insects imbibe nutrients while feeding which are currently of unclear benefit to them. However, the females do not engage in "puddling" behaviours, and confine their diet strictly to flower nectar.

Family PIERIDAE

Butterflies of the family Pieridae may be encountered in all of the habitats and altitudes present in Costa Rica. The more familiar species of Costa Rican Pieridae are usually white, yellow or orange in colouration, and are great lovers of sunshine. Their colours serve to create the common reference to these insects as being "Whites" and "Sulphurs".

As is the case with the family Papilionidae, males of Pierid species also drink water from dampened earth, especially that which is moistened by urine. Some males, such as those of *Catasticta* butterflies, may partially emerse themselves in the running water of the rivers and streams of their montane habitats while engaging in this behaviour.

The eggs of Pierids are usually spindle shaped, and may be deposited singly or in clusters of variable sizes, depending upon the species in question. Important hostplants for Pierid larvae in Costa Rica include *Cassia* (Caesalpinaceae), Mistletoes (Loranthaceae), members of the pea family (Fabaceae) and Brassicas (Brassicaceae). Generally, the larvae of this family are very cryptic, and may be difficult to locate upon their hostplants.

Most Pierid larvae are smooth in appearance, and lack spines or other armatures, although the larvae of gregarious species, such as those of the genus *Catasticta*, possess hairs and are quite conspicuous upon their hostplants.

The pupae of this family are usually well camouflaged, and coloured in shades of green or brown. Pupae of Pierids are formed with a silken girdle placed around the body, in the same manner as the family Papilionidae.

Common Costa Rican representatives of this family include *Phoebis philea*, *Phoebis argante*, *Phoebis sennae*, *Appias drusilla*, and *Ascia monuste*.

Subfamily COLIADINAE

Members of the subfamily Coliadinae are found around the world, in environments that range from arctic wastes to tropical rainforests. Most species of the Coliadinae are white, yellow or orange in colouration, and are familiar Costa Rican butterflies, which are commonly observed even in the streets of San José. These insects are powerful fliers, which may periodically participate in huge migrations.

Members of the Coliadinae are strongly attracted to the colour red, as the author discovered after being bombarded by these butterflies while wearing a t-shirt of that colour. This garment was apparently mistaken for a large red flower, such as Hibiscus, which serves as a popular nectar source for these insects.

Familiar examples of Costa Rican Coliadinae include species of the genera *Phoebis* and *Anteos*. Members of this subfamily fly throughout the year in Costa Rica.

Subfamily DISMORPHIINAE

Representatives of this subfamily are virtually confined to the tropical areas of the New World, and are excellent mimics of a variety of toxic butterflies. Not only wing colourations and patternings are duplicated convincingly by these insects, but also the generally slow and flapping flight behaviours of the different model species.

The favoured habitats of these butterflies are shaded forests, where the insects are usually encountered as solitary individuals flying amongst their commoner models. However, certain species exist only at high altitudes, in such situations as the peaks of Costa Rica's volcanoes and mountains.

Subfamily PIERINAE

The subfamily Pierinae occurs throughout much of the world, with representatives of it being found at all elevations, and in all environments in Costa Rica. Many species are very common in their given habitats, for example the varieties of *Catasticta* butterflies which congregate in large groups in order to drink at water seepages. The familiar cabbage butterflies (*Pieris rapae*), the larvae of which plague vegetable gardens throughout temperate regions of the world, also belong to this subfamily.

Common species of the Pierinae which fly in Costa Rica include *Ascia monuste*, *Appias drusilla*, and at medium to higher altitudes, the genus *Catasticta*. These butterflies are generally strong fliers, which are most active during sunny weather. The larvae of Costa Rican Pierinae utilize hostplants such as Mistletoes (Loranthaceae) and various Brassicas (Brassicaceae). They may feed solitarily or gregariously, depending upon the species in question.

CHAPTER IV

WHERE TO LOOK FOR
BUTTERFLIES IN COSTA RICA

Due to its extremely varied geographical relief, and the prevailing winds from the Caribbean and Pacific sides of the country, many different vegetational zones and localized climates have developed for butterflies to utilize in Costa Rica.

Because of the variety of habitats which are present to explore, the visitor to Costa Rica would be well advised to plan ahead, so that the butterflies and other fauna, flora, and scenery of these different regions may be enjoyed to their fullest extent (Map 1).

Map 1   A map of Costa Rica, showing the different provinces and major centers of population.

By far the most productive areas in which to search for butterflies in Costa Rica are the rainforest habitats which exist in the lowlands and mid-elevational zones of the Atlantic sector of the country. There is persistent and often heavy precipitation in these areas, which serves to provide a wide range of vegetation on a constant basis, due to the lack of a true "dry season". Butterflies in such areas have the luxury of being able to breed perpetually throughout the balance of the year.

In contrast to the lush zones mentioned above, there are seasonally dry regions adjacent to Costa Rica's Pacific coastline. In such areas, many species of butterflies may cease to breed for several months during the dry seasons. Other butterflies may migrate on a seasonal basis across the mountains which divide the country, in order to temporarily colonize "greener pastures" on the Atlantic side of these ranges.

There are no better places to seek butterflies than in the thirty four National Parks and reserves that are distributed throughout Costa Rica (Map 2). Although some of these areas do not as of yet possess well developed facilities for visitors in the form of lodging and infrastructure, they usually contain accessible trails which are excellent for the purposes of butterfly watching, and enjoying a variety of other flora and fauna. Because of the large market which exists in Costa Rica for ecotourism, most of these parks and reserves have tourist facilities located in close proximity to their boundaries.

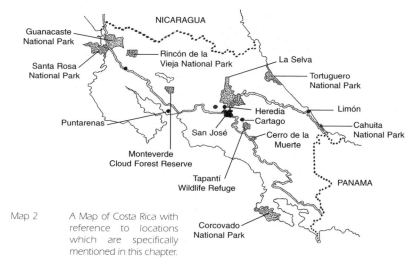

Map 2   A Map of Costa Rica with reference to locations which are specifically mentioned in this chapter.

A logical plan seems to have been followed with regard to the selection of habitats that Costa Rica's National Parks represent. As a result, the majority of the country's life zones, and the concomitant biodiversity that is possessed in each, are preserved to some degree. In addition to National Parks, there are also national and private reserves in Costa Rica, many of which are very extensive.

Some of the private reserves, such as La Selva, which is administered by the Organization for Tropical Studies, lie adjacent to National Park areas. In the case of La Selva, it is situated in direct proximity to Braulio Carrillo National Park, and constitutes a large and important buffer zone of protected land in addition to that contained within the boundaries of the park itself.

Other highlights that the National Parks offer is some of the most spectacular scenery to be experienced in the country. Several parks feature volcanoes as focal points, many of which are active. Chirripó, the highest peak in Costa Rica, at 3820 meters in elevation, is situated within the Chirripó National Park of, which is over 50,000 hectares in area. The lush green canals which lie along the north eastern coastline of Costa Rica fall within the boundaries of Tortuguero National Park. Tortuguero's beaches also provide important nesting areas for turtles, such as the highly endangered Green Sea Turtle. There are obviously many worthwhile experiences to be had from visiting such areas, besides seeking the butterflies which reside within them.

North and East of San José

Braulio Carrillo National Park

Braulio Carrillo National Park lies within easy reach of San José, and is an excellent location in which to observe butterflies. This park is over 108,000 acres in size, and is composed of several habitats, including lowland rainforest and a variety of montane tropical forest zones.

There are trails leading from the park headquarters which may be utilized for observing butterflies. During periods of heavy rain, the highway which runs through the park may be slick, foggy, and treacherous. This is a thought to consider when planning an excursion there during such conditions.

The scenery of Braulio Carrillo includes rugged mountains, hills and valleys. It is densely clothed in largely unexplored rainforest, and provides one of the most impressive vistas to be experienced anywhere in the world.

Located almost at the northern boundary of Braulio Carrillo, when driving north towards Limón, is the Rainforest Aerial Tram. This is a system of cable cars which provides one with a chance to ride above, and through sections of the rainforest canopy itself. The Aerial Tram provides an excellent means by which to observe the many species of butterflies and other creatures which live exclusively in the treetops. *Morpho* species, in particular *Morpho theseus*, commonly fly at this location. This ride also allows one to view the huge variety of other flora and fauna that call the rainforest canopy home.

La Selva Biological Reserve

By continuing on from Braulio Carrillo, and then west along the highway toward the town of Puerto Viejo de Sarapiquí, one soon arrives at La Selva Biological Reserve, which is comprised of over 3,500 acres of primary forest.

La Selva has an extremely high diversity of butterflies flying within its boundaries. It also offers facilities to those who are interested in learning more about tropical ecology. Excursions there with a camera and some patience will result in many wonderful photographs and memories.

Individuals who are interested in birds will also enjoy the huge variety of species which may be spotted at La Selva. This reserve provides the visitor with an excellent introduction to the lowland rainforests of the Sarapiquí region in which it is located.

Tortuguero and Cahuita National Parks

If one backtracks from La Selva and continues north and east towards the city of Limón on the Caribbean Coast, there are two National Parks of particular interest to be visited, namely Tortuguero and Cahuita.

To the north of Limón is Tortuguero National Park, which is over 46,000 acres in size. This park is best explored via the system of inland canals that wind through it. As mentioned previously, the park contains beaches which are vitally important nesting sites for the Green Sea Turtle. Within the park itself, hiking and camping are permitted, and there are facilities and lodges available for travellers in the village of Tortuguero, and also adjacently to the park itself.

Cahuita National Park is located to the south of the city of Limón, in close proximity to the Panamanian border. Cahuita is extremely beautiful, and is easily accessible from the town of Cahuita itself, where there are good facilities that may be made use of by visitors.

There are well maintained trails within the park which may be utilized by butterfly watchers, and beautiful beaches where one can sooth sore feet in the warm waters of the Caribbean. Large populations of *Morpho peleides* fly at Cahuita. These butterflies are easy to observe while they sail along the main trail which runs adjacently to the beach itself. *Caligo* species are also common at Cahuita, in particular *Caligo atreus* and also other members of the subfamily Brassolinae, such as *Opsiphanes cassina*.

An excursion to the Caribbean coast of Costa Rica also gives one the chance to experience the friendly and accepting culture of the inhabitants of this area.

The Orosi Valley

Within a days return distance from San José lies the Orosi Valley, which is easily accessible by road via the city of Cartago. The area surrounding the town of Cachí, which is located in this valley, was studied in great detail with regard to its butterfly fauna by the naturalist William Schaus. Butterflies which he collected in the vicinity of Cachí during the early part of the twentieth century now reside in many of the worlds museums.

The montane forests which stand in this valley are rich in butterflies. One of the best places in which to observe butterflies in the Orosi Valley is the Tapantí Wildlife Refuge. This refuge is open to the public throughout the week, and contains many trails that are excellent for the purposes of observing butterflies, birds and other flora and fauna. It is advisable to hire an experienced guide if possible while visiting Tapantí, as the forest is quite thick, and it can be a simple matter to lose ones way when exploring there.

Butterfly species which are commonly observed in the atlantic lowland and mid-elevational forest areas described above are *Morpho peleides*, *Morpho cypris*, *Heliconius erato*, *Heliconius cydno*, *Heliconius hecale*, *Dryas iulia*, *Papilio thoas*, *Parides iphidamas*, *Siproeta stenes*, *Caligo eurilochus* and *Phoebis philea*.

Most of these species, plus many others, should be easily observed in the space of a few days, within or adjacent to suitable forest habitats that exist in the above locations.

West of San José

The Pacific sector of Costa Rica possess a butterfly fauna which is more affected by climatic change than that of the eastern zones of the country. This is due to the occurrence of very pronounced dry seasons, especially in the province of Guanacaste. As a result, the appearances of a variety of butterflies in this region of Costa Rica is directly linked to the presence or absence of rain. Many butterflies appear to migrate seasonally to and from the western zones of Costa Rica, seeming to follow the most beneficial climate to be had at the time. Rains generally fall here from the end of April until the beginning of November, after which ensues a season of drought. Formerly lush areas often dry up entirely, creating an extremely arid environment which is devoid of most of the butterflies which were resident there during the wet season.

Santa Rosa National Park

In the north-west of Guanacaste province lies Santa Rosa National Park, which has an interesting butterfly fauna that is observed to its best advantage shortly after the seasonal rains begin to fall in May. Santa Rosa is easily accessible by road via the city of Liberia, and is one of the most popular National Parks visited by tourists. There are areas of seasonal dry forest to be enjoyed there, as well as numerous beaches which are frequented by Olive Ridley turtles.

Guanacaste National Park

On the opposite side of the Pan American Highway from Santa Rosa is Guanacaste National Park, which serves as an important corridor for the migrations of butterflies, birds and other fauna that pass through this area between the dry and wet seasons. The Orosi and Cacao Volcanoes within its boundaries both bear evergreen and cloud forest habitats upon their slopes, which are environments that have now fortunately been protected as a result of the creation of this park.

Rincón de la Vieja National Park

In close proximity to Guanacaste National Park is Rincón de la Vieja National Park. This park is rich in butterflies which are typical of pacific evergreen forest environments, such as *Caligo memnon*, and *Morpho peleides*. Also included in the butterfly fauna of Rincón de la Vieja is the huge white *Morpho polyphemus*, which is endemic within Costa Rica to the slopes of the Santa María and Rincón de la Vieja volcanoes, both of which are located within the park boundaries.

The Monteverde Cloud Forest Reserve

While visiting the province of Puntarenas, the Monteverde Cloud Forest Reserve, and the vicinity which surrounds it, is definitely worth exploring for its butterflies. Many species of butterflies utilize the Tilarán Mountains in which Monteverde is situated as a corridor for seasonal migrations. As a result, a great variety of resident and transitory species may be observed there.

The Reserve itself is composed of thick, primary, high elevation forest (fig. 4.1), which often makes observing the butterflies that inhabit it difficult to accomplish at times. Butterflies are much easier to observe in the Monteverde area along the many roads and trails that surround the Reserve itself.

Fig. 4.1   The Monteverde Cloud Forest Reserve.

Many of the butterflies which fly at Monteverde become active only during periods of sunshine, which may be infrequent in areas of cloud forest. However, with some luck and patience, species such as *Morpho peleides* may be encountered, as well as other typical higher altitude species such as *Heliconius clysonymus*. Several varieties of the genus *Marpesia* fly there, with these particular butterflies appearing to use the Tilarán Mountains as a corridor for seasonal migrations. During such movements, *Marpesias* may sometimes be observed while flying and nectaring in the thousands. Rarities, such as *Papilio garamas syedra* haunt the ridgetops of the Tilarán Mountains. This butterfly may be observed while gliding slowly around the tops of the tallest trees at Monteverde during periods of sunshine.

Areas of evergreen forest exist on the Pacific side of the central mountain ranges, and extend from the city of Puntarenas to the border with Panamá. Such habitats contain relatively stable communities of butterflies which are not as dramatically affected by seasonal weather patterns as is the case of areas in the province of Guanacaste.

Corcovado National Park

Corcovado National Park, located upon the Osa Península, is an excellent place in which to observe butterflies that are typical of tropical wet forest habitats. However, Corcovado lacks the sufficient infrastructure which would permit ready access to its butterfly fauna, and is an area which must be almost exclusively explored upon by foot.

Both the heat and humidity are high throughout the year at Corcovado, and a majority of the insects and other creatures that can make life uncomfortable for the traveller seem to abound there. However, for more adventurous souls, the rich variety of life that may be appreciated at Corcovado will serve as a just reward for the occasional discomforts associated with visiting it.

Corcovado contains a great variety of butterfly species, with typical representatives including *Morpho peleides*, *Morpho cypris*, *Morpho theseus*, *Caligo atreus* and *Siproeta steneles*.

The Talamancan Mountains

The higher elevation forests of the Atlantic and Pacific slopes of the Talamancan Mountain Range are a fascinating area in which to seek butterflies. There are many resident species of butterflies which inhabit the Talamancas, with certain varieties being exclusive residents of the cloud forests which exist between the elevations of 1,400 to 3,000 meters.

Cerro de la Muerte

The region surrounding Cerro de la Muerte is quite accessible to the traveller, and possesses several tourist lodges that are situated within its vicinity. These lodges provide excellent bases from which to range out in order to search for butterflies, and also birds. Frequently observed amongst the latter is the famous and spectacular Resplendent Quetzal.

Butterflies of particular interest which occur within the cloud forests of the Talamancas are *Papilio garamas syedra*, *Dione moneta*, *Catasticta* species and *Anetia thirza insignis*. The latter species is a very interesting relative of the Monarch butterfly (*Danaus plexippus*).

The Central Valley

The Central Valley, in which San José is situated, is home to a great variety of butterflies throughout the year. There are also many additional species which use this valley as a corridor for travel between dry and wet areas on a seasonal basis. Representative butterflies of the Central Valley include *Phoebis philea*, *Phoebis sennae*, *Ascia monuste*, *Dryas iulia*, *Dione vanillae*, *Papilio thoas*, *Papilio anchisiades*, *Anartia fatima*, *Chlosyne janais*, *Heliconius erato*, *Siproeta steneles*, and the Monarch butterfly (*Danaus plexippus*).

Butterflies which inhabit the Central Valley often occupy environments which have been heavily affected by the large human population that exists there. However, species such as those indicated above seem to prosper in such conditions, as their larval foodplants usually grow well in disturbed habitats.

How to Search More Effectively for Costa Rican Butterflies

Unlike the butterflies which occur in temperate zones of the world, tropical butterflies are seemingly more specialized as to where and when they make their appearances during the day. In addition to this, they are usually quite specific with regard to the microhabitats that they prefer to exist in within their general environments.

Knowledge that the author has accumulated with regard to the behaviours of Costa Rican butterflies has been of much use to him, enabling more effective studies and photography of a variety of these insects to be accomplished in a wide range of different habitats.

At this juncture, it would seem logical that some insights pertaining to the habits of some of these butterflies would be of assistance to individuals who may not be aware of such information. In this section, the author wishes to provide the reader with some relevant information that will hopefully provide more success with regard to their efforts while working in the field.

Morpho Butterflies

A case in point as relates to the individual behaviours of butterfly species would be those of *Morpho* butterflies, which seem to exhibit very regimented hours of flight activity. Males of *Morpho peleides* prefer to fly from the mid-morning until approximately noon. Conversely, the females of the same species are most active from noon until about 2 p.m, when they are frequently observed while seeking out, and ovipositing upon their hostplants. The males of *Morpho amathonte* typically fly from dawn until the mid-morning, with the females of the same species being active from noon until mid-afternoon, when they are ovipositing.

In the case of the spectacular *Morpho cypris*, the males are on the wing from late morning until the mid-afternoon. The author has observed many male specimens of *Morpho cypris* feeding on rotting fruits that were utilized as baits. Indeed, it would appear that the males of *Morpho cypris* feed from fruits at the same time on a daily basis, usually appearing quite punctually at two-thirty in the afternoon.

A further detail to be addressed with regard to the habits of *Morpho* butterflies is the height at which individual species fly. *Morpho cypris* is typically a high flier, which is most often observed many meters up in the canopies and subcanopies of rainforests. In contrast, *Morpho peleides* is observed at the level of a meter or so above the ground along forest edges in usual circumstances. However, a rarer but similar relative of *Morpho peleides*, *Morpho granadensis*, is usually encountered while flying low along the streams and dimly lit trails within the forest interior of the habitats it shares with *Morpho peleides*. Although *Morpho granadensis* usually flies at the same height as *Morpho peleides*, it utilizes more foliage as cover while active than its more common counterpart.

The distinctive areas of the forests in which these *Morpho* butterflies exist are referred to as **microhabitats,** that is, smaller habitats which may be utilized individually by different organisms within a larger environment.

The habits such as those of Costa Rican *Morpho* species serve as excellent illustrations of how different, and often closely related butterfly species regulate their behaviours in order to more effectively share the same habitats. By confining their different activities to specific times during the day, such species tend to interact less frequently. Each variety of *Morpho* appears to possess its own environmental niche, which is generally not utilized by other species within the same genus.

Prospecting Tropical Forests: Some Details to Consider

While exploring rainforests, it is always a good practice to pay close attention to the forest floor. Quite frequently, a tiny patch of pink will sail into view, and gently settle upon a leaf or log. Upon closer inspection, this colouration will be seen to belong to a Glasswinged Satyr (*Cithaerias menander*), which is a delicate and exquisite member of the subfamily Satyrinae. The wings of this butterfly are transparent, and pigmented only with deep pink patches and small occelli upon its hindwings.

When prospecting forest edges, it is worthwhile to look up and pay attention to tree trunks which are facing the sun. Such locations are frequently utilized as perches for individuals of *Hamadryas* species, which are popularly referred to as "Cracker Butterflies". This name stems from the crackling sounds that these butterflies produce while in flight. These sounds are very reminiscent of the rapid clicking noises that one would experience when hearing static electricity. *Hamadryas* butterflies rest upon their perches with their heads facing downwards, and press their wings firmly against the bark of chosen trees (fig. 4.2). This behaviour, together with their wing patterning and colouration, creates for these insects an extremely effective means of concealment.

Fig. 4.2 A *Hamadryas* butterfly in its typical resting pose upon a tree trunk.

Many other butterflies which frequent the edges of forests may be observed while perching upon, or flying around foliage at the height of one or two meters above the ground. Butterflies which are encountered along forest edges are frequently individuals that have descended from the forest canopy in order to search for oviposition sites. *Heliconius erato*, *Heliconius cydno* and *Heliconius hecale* are commonly seen while flying delicately amongst the greenery in such situations, as are *Morpho peleides*, *Siproeta steneles*, *Siproeta epaphus*, and *Parides iphidamas*.

By walking in the interior of the forest, approximately two meters in parallel to an open trail, many butterflies which prefer the shadier conditions of the forest understory may be observed. Those commonly encountered in such conditions will include many members of the subfamilies Ithomiinae and Satyrinae.

It is also of benefit to pay attention to different types of fruits which may have fallen to the forest floor. In particular, the fermenting fruits of a variety of palms are extremely attractive to many butterflies as a food source. *Morpho*, *Caligo*, *Archaeoprepona* and other species of the family Nymphalidae are strongly attracted to such fruits as banana and mango.

Indeed, butterflies which feed upon fermenting fruits often become quite intoxicated in the process, which makes approaching them for the purposes of observation easier than would normally be the case. Such situations also provide excellent opportunities for photography, should one be so inclined.

Another extremely popular butterfly food source to be aware of is dung, typically that of species of carnivores which also exist in forest habitats. The author has frequently been quite amazed by the great variety of species, represented by many different families and genera of butterflies, that respond to such lures in the rainforests of Costa Rica. At times, butterflies will appear to examine, and subsequently feed at such baits literally minutes after they have been set.

A pair of binoculars may often be extremely useful in order to view canopy species in forest habitats. The spectacular black and yellow Garamas Swallowtail (*Papilio garamas syedra*) (Fig. 4.3) is best observed by this means in its cloud forest habitats. Individuals of this species rarely descend to the ground, being more at home whilst perching, and occasionally sailing in slow circles, around the uppermost reaches of emergent canopy trees.

An observer who takes into account simple advice such as that suggested above, may enjoy more success than one who is aware of such small details. The primary guidelines involve keeping ones eyes open in **all** directions, and to attempt to work through any given habitat through the course of a full day, if at all possible. By adhering to the latter point, many observations will be made of species that may only be active at specific times, and which would otherwise have been missed.

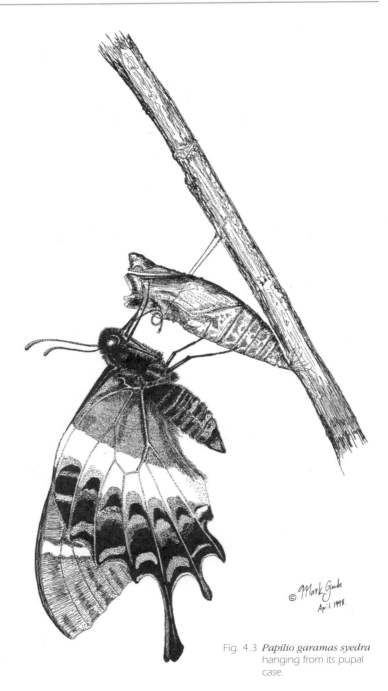

Fig. 4.3 *Papilio garamas syedra* hanging from its pupal case.

PLATE 1

Mullerian Mimicry(co-mimicry)

1. *Heliconius hecale zuleika* ....page 66
2. *Melinaea ethra lilis*
3. *Heliconius cydno galanthus* ....page 65
4. *Heliconius sapho leuce*
5. *Heliconius erato petiverana* ....page 66
6. *Heliconius melpomene rosina*

Batesian Mimicry

7. *Parides iphidamas iphidamas* (model) ....page 80
8. *Papilio anchisiades idaeus* (mimic) ....page 79

PLATE 2

PLATE 3

PLATE 4

PLATE 5

PLATE 6

1. *Catonephele numilia esite* (upper surface of male)............................page 72
2. *Catonephele numilia esite* (upper surface of female)........................page 72
3. *Hamadryas amphinome mexicana* (upper surface of male)............page 73
4. *Siproeta steneles biplagiata* (upper surface of female)......................page 75
5. *Mechanitis polymnia isthmia* (upper surface of male).......................page 67
6. *Eueides aliphera aliphera* (upper surface of male)............................page 64
7. *Heliconiuis charitonius* (upper surface of male)................................page 65
8. *Danaus plexippus* (upper surface of female)....................................page 63
9. *Dryas iulia* (upper surface of male)..page 64
10. *Chlosyne janais* (upper surface of female).......................................page 72
11. *Lycorea cleobaea atergatis* (upper surface of female)......................page 63
12. *Marpesia merops* (upper surface of male)..page 73
13. *Nessaea aglaura* (upper surface of female).......................................page 74
14. *Biblis hyperia* (upper surface of male)..page 71
15. *Adelpha cytheraea marcia* (upper surface of male).........................page 71
16. *Anartia fatima* (upper surface of female)..page 71

CHAPTER V

SPECIES ACCOUNTS

Family:	NYMPHALIDAE
Subfamily:	BRASSOLINAE
Species:	*Caligo atreus* Plate 2
Distribution:	*Caligo atreus* is widely distributed from southern Mexico to Ecuador and Venezuela in a variety of different subspecies. It is represented by subspecies *dionysos* in Costa Rica.
Larval foodplants:	The larvae of *Caligo atreus* utilize *Heliconia* (Heliconiaceae), Banana (Musaceae), and occasionally species of ornamental Gingers (Zingiberaceae) as foodplants.
General information:	This magnificent species is commonly encountered in the rainforests of the Atlantic and wetter Pacific areas of Costa Rica. The rich purple and yellow upperside coloration of *Caligo atreus* makes the identification of this species easy, and distinguishes it from other members of its genus while in flight.

The butterflies typically fly at dusk, as is the general rule of *Caligo* species. However, these insects may be active during the day in shaded areas within forests and secondary growth, where individuals may often be observed whilst they feed upon a variety of fallen fruits in the company of other butterflies.

The females of this species oviposit during the late afternoons and evenings, leaving single or small clusters of eggs on both sides of the leaves of the hostplant, and sometimes upon the stems. The eggs are round, white, are finely sculpted with vertical ribbing, and develop a purplish band around their tops if they are fertile. These eggs hatch within twelve days and the resultant larvae change in appearance with each molt. The mature larvae are huge, often exceeding 12 centimeters in length, and are coloured in brown and olive green, with black and reddish brown markings. Pupae of *Caligo atreus* hang by the tail, are stocky, golden yellow in colouration, and possess mottled brown markings on their wing cases. Emergence of the butterflies usually takes place between twenty to thirty days after pupation.

Family:	NYMPHALIDAE
Subfamily:	BRASSOLINAE
Species:	*Caligo eurilochus* Plate 2
Distribution:	*Caligo eurilochus* occurs in southern Mexico and throughout much of Central and South America. A number of subspecies exist, with subspecies *sulanus* occurring in Costa Rica.
Larval foodplants:	This species utilizes many types of *Heliconia* (Heliconiaceae) and Banana (Musaceae) as larval hostplants.

General information: *Caligo eurilochus* is a huge and impressive butterfly which occurs commonly throughout much of Costa Rica in forest habitats of up to 1,000 meters or more in elevation. The adults fly powerfully, but are easily baited by the use of fermenting bananas. Females of this butterfly are gigantic, and are amongst the largest butterflies to be found in Costa Rica.

The white, round eggs are deposited in clusters upon the hostplant. These eggs develop into huge brown larvae, which are often encountered in large aggregations that are composed of several different instars. As is usual with the genus *Caligo*, a large percentage of the eggs of this species are parasitized by Trichogrammatid wasps.

Family: NYMPHALIDAE
Subfamily: BRASSOLINAE
Species: *Caligo memnon*   Figure 5.1
Distribution: *Caligo memnon* is distributed from southern Mexico to Peru and Amazonia, with subspecies *memnon* flying in Costa Rica.

Fig 5.1   A newly emerged adult of *Caligo memnon* (Brassolinae), next to its empty pupal case.

Larval foodplants: This butterfly completes its larval development upon species of Banana (Musaceae), and *Heliconia* (Heliconiaceae).

General Information: This familiar species is commonly met with in the Pacific zone of Costa Rica. However, it may be also encountered quite frequently in the Central Valley, particularly during times of seasonal rain. The butterflies are frequently discovered while at rest in banana patches during the day, even in heavily urbanized areas such as San José. The creamy colour of the forewings of this species is a very distinctive field character by which to identify this species from others of the same genus while in flight. As is usual with most of the Brassolinae, *Caligo memnon* is strongly attracted by fermenting fruits as an adult food source, and to rotting bananas in particular.

The huge brown larvae of this butterfly may be discovered in large clusters upon the leaves and trunks of cultivated bananas. The author has counted as many as seventy individuals, comprised of many different instars, resting together beneath a single banana leaf. When these larvae reach the fifth instar, they seem to prefer to reside upon the trunk of the tree, sometimes communally, where their cryptic colouration conceals them most effectively. Larvae of this species feed principally at night and then digest their meals over the course of the following day.

The pupae are very large, stocky, and cryptically coloured in brown or grey (Fig. 3.2). They hang by the tail from a suitable support, usually in dense undergrowth. The butterflies eclose approximately three weeks after pupation takes place.

Family:	NYMPHALIDAE
Subfamily:	BRASSOLINAE
Species:	*Opsiphanes cassina* Plate 4
Distribution:	This species occurs from southern Mexico to much of South America in a variety of subspecies. In Costa Rica, two subspecies occur, namely *chiriquensis* and *fabricii*.
Larval foodplants:	Many varieties of palms (Arecaceae) are used by *Opsiphanes cassina* for larval development.
General information:	This common species occurs in forests and disturbed habitats throughout Costa Rica. At Cahuita National Park, and other costal areas where palms are particularly common, the author has frequently observed females of this butterfly ovipositing in the late afternoons upon a variety of different species of these trees. The eggs are round, chalky white in colour, and are usually deposited singly at the bases of palm fronds. The females will be observed to carefully probe with their ovipositors until they find a suitable location for each egg. Eggs are quite easy to locate if the plants are carefully searched. As is common with the sub-family Brassolinae, many eggs perish due to the actions of parasitic wasps of the family Trichogrammatidae.

When young, the larvae construct a shelter in which to hide by folding over a section of the palm frond that they are feeding upon. The large mature larva is green, finely striped lengthwise with yellow lines, and has a brown head capsule which is adorned with straight horns.

Pupae of this species are stocky, brown or green in colour, and possess small silver spots upon their wing cases. The author has discovered many dead pupae upon palm trees. These were festooned with holes that were manufactured by the larvae of parasites which had exited the pupae in question. The butterflies are extremely swift flyers, and are strongly attracted to food sources such as dung or rotting fruits.

• •

Family:	NYMPHALIDAE
Subfamily:	CHARAXINAE
Species:	*Prepona omphale* Figure 1.13
Distribution:	This insect is widely distributed from southern Mexico to Central America and throughout much of South America. It is represented by many subspecies, with the subspecies octavia occurring in Costa Rica.
Larval foodplants:	Species of the family Mimosaceae, of which common varieties are *Inga* species.
General information:	This species is a common resident of forest and adjacent secondary-growth habitats throughout Costa Rica. These butterflies are extremely powerful fliers, and are by nature quite nervous with regard to settling upon their food sources. Fermenting fruits or dung will often be "scouted out" several times before the butterflies will alight to feed. This behaviour may be punctuated with periodic rests, with the head of the insect pointing downwards, from high up on nearby branches or tree trunks. This behaviour often leaves the observer with the impression that they are being "watched". Once feeding is initiated, the butterflies may be quite easily approached if care is taken to avoid sudden movements. The use of baits is by far the most effective method by which to observe this insect more closely. The bright bluish-green upperside colouration is hidden while the insect feeds, being replaced by very cryptic and leaf-like brown underside markings, which provide excellent concealment.

The females deposit their round, white eggs singly upon the undersurfaces of young leaves of the hostplant. The mature larva is a peculiar creature, that is cryptically patterned in brown, with two long tails projecting from its terminal body segment. Its head is triangular in shape, with two horns which face backwards. Larvae of this species possess very thin segments adjacent to their heads, which gives them the appearance of having a "neck". Pupae of this butterfly hang by the tail, are ovoid in shape, and light green in colour.

These butterflies appear to be quite territorial, as individuals which are observed through binoculars will be commonly seen to utilize the same tree trunks as perches for several consecutive days. While perching, the adults typically rest with their heads pointing downwards, and their wings opened slightly, which displays a fraction of their blue and black upperside colouration. They may leave these perches periodically in order to engage in brief soaring flights around adjacent trees and vegetation in order to pursue other butterflies, and occasionally small birds.

Family:	NYMPHALIDAE
Subfamily:	DANAINAE
Species:	*Danaus plexippus* Plate 6
Distribution:	This species flies throughout much of North, Central and South America. It is a great wanderer, that is capable of travelling great distances. Individuals of the North American summer populations are occasionally observed in the British Isles during the Autumn, when they occasionally stray from their migration route to Mexico. *Danaus plexippus* also flies in many regions of Asia and Australasia, where ever suitable hostplants occur.
Larval foodplants:	Various species of Milkweeds (*Asclepias*) are hostplants of this species, and in particular *Asclepias curassavica*.
General information:	*Danaus plexippus*, popularly known as the Monarch Butterfly, is a familiar Costa Rican species which occurs throughout the country in association with its larval hostplants. *Asclepias* species are common weeds which grow well even in poor soils, and benefit greatly from the open areas that are created by human activities.

These butterflies have a slow, sailing flight, and may be observed while nectaring upon a variety of flowers, including *Lantana*, and also those that are produced by the hostplants. The females deposit their small, white eggs upon many parts of the hostplant, including its leaves and flowers. Eggs of this species may be easily located by passively searching a few *Asclepias* plants. The yellow, white and black striped larvae of this butterfly are extremely conspicuous while feeding upon their foodplants (Fig. 3.3). Larvae of *Danaus plexippus* grow extremely rapidly, and often complete their development in under two weeks time. The pupae are suspended by the tail, are coloured in a beautiful jade green, and are ornamented with small metallic gold spots. The Costa Rican populations of this species appear to be resident ones, and do not participate in the immense yearly migrations that have made the North American populations famous.

• •

Family:	NYMPHALIDAE
Subfamily:	DANAINAE
Species:	*Lycorea cleobaea* Plate 6
Distribution:	*Lycorea cleobaea* occurs commonly from southern México to Bolivia. Subspecies *atergatis* flies in Costa Rica.
Larval foodplants:	Females of *Lycorea cleobaea* lay their eggs upon species of *Ficus* (Moraceae).
General information:	This conspicuous and common species is a familiar sight within forests and along forest edges throughout much of Costa Rica. The author has not frequently observed this butterfly in full sunlight, as the insects seem to prefer shadier conditions. The male possesses two large eversable brushes at the tip of its abdomen which are utilized to convey pheromones during courtship, and may also be deployed if the insects are handled. The butterflies are commonly observed at nectar sources such as *Lantana*, and possess a strong, sailing flight. Larvae of *Lycorea cleobaea* are ringed in black and white, and are quite conspicuous upon their hostplants.

Family:	NYMPHALIDAE
Subfamily:	HELICONIINAE
Species:	*Dryas iulia* Plate 6
Distribution:	*Dryas iulia* flies in the southern United States, throughout the Caribbean Islands, Mexico, and much of Central and South America.
Larval foodplants:	Many species of Passiflora (Passifloraceae) are consumed by the larvae of *Dryas iulia*, but the most popular choices in the experience of the author are *Passiflora vitifolia* and *Passiflora biflora*.
General information:	This familiar flame-orange species is very common throughout Costa Rica, wherever its *Passiflora* hostplants occur. These butterflies are extremely strong and well-controlled fliers. They may be frequently observed whilst nectaring upon a variety of flowers, a particular favourite of which is *Lantana*. The author has observed individuals of this species returning to specific patches of Lantana for several consecutive days, which illustrates that the butterflies are often quite faithful to their sources of nourishment.

Females of *Dryas iulia* oviposit whenever there is strong sun. They are often observed whilst fluttering amongst tangled vegetation that lies upon the ground in open areas and along forest edges, in search of their *Passiflora* hostplants. When a suitable plant is located, a single yellow egg is deposited upon the tips of new growth, the tendrils, or sometimes upon twigs and vegetation which are adjacent to the foodplant. In the latter scenario, the larvae are forced to wander in search of their hostplants. The author has observed this species ovipositing upon *Passiflora biflora* at Cahuita National Park, where both the hostplants and butterflies are extremely common.

Larvae of *Dryas iulia* are mottled in shades of brown, and have black and white spines. The pupae are also coloured in shades of brown, and are typical of the family in form. However, these pupae are less ornate and much smoother than those of the genus *Heliconius*, and closely resemble bird droppings. This butterfly flies abundantly throughout the year, and may be readily observed by visitors to Costa Rica.

• •

Family:	NYMPHALIDAE
Subfamily:	HELICONIINAE
Species:	*Eueides aliphera* Plate 6
Distribution:	This butterfly occurs commonly from southern Mexico to the Amazon Basin.
Larval Foodplants:	A variety of *Passiflora* species (Passifloraceae) are utilized by this species as larval hosts, with a favourite in the experience of the author being *Passiflora vitifolia*.
General Information:	This familiar species is usually met with along forest edges throughout much of Costa Rica. It resembles a miniature of the related species *Dryas iulia*, with which it is frequently found, and often shares hostplants. The latter species usually chooses to deposit its eggs upon the tips of the hostplant's tendrils, whereas *Eueides aliphera* prefers to oviposit upon the undersurfaces of the leaves of the same plants.

These butterflies visit a variety of flowers, and are easy to approach and observe.

• •

Family:	NYMPHALIDAE
Subfamily:	HELICONIINAE
Species:	*Heliconius charitonius*　　　Plate 6
Distribution:	This butterfly occurs in the southern United States, the Caribbean, and throughout much of Central and South America.
Larval foodplants:	The author has located larvae of this butterfly feeding upon species of *Passiflora* (Passifloraceae) such as *Passiflora biflora* and *Passiflora menispermifolia*.
General information:	This butterfly is a familiar sight throughout Costa Rica, and may be observed to elevations of 1,000 meters or more. It thrives in areas which have been created by human activities, such as shrubby and weedy secondary growth habitats, and is a common sight even in the city of San José. The bold yellow and black colouration and slow flight of *Heliconius charitonius* make it unmistakable and easy to identify.

Females of this species deposit their yellow eggs upon the young leaves of the chosen foodplants, which grow commonly along forest edges. The mature larvae are white, spotted with black dots, and are adorned with long black spines. These larvae produce pupae which are typical of the genus in structure and colouration. The butterflies eclose approximately 12 to 14 days following pupation.

• •

Family:	NYMPHALIDAE
Subfamily:	HELICONIINAE
Species:	*Heliconius cydno*　　　Plate 1
Distribution:	*Heliconius cydno* occurs from southern Mexico to Ecuador in a variety of different subspecies. The subspecies *chioneus* and *galanthus* fly in Costa Rica.
Larval foodplants:	The author has located larvae of this butterfly upon a variety of *Passiflora* species (Passifloraceae), but most commonly *Passiflora biflora* and *Passiflora vitifolia*.
General information:	This common black and white butterfly is a typical inhabitant of forest habitats throughout much of the Atlantic side of Costa Rica, to elevations of 1,000 meters or more. The subspecies *galanthus* flies in much of the Costa Rican range of this species. A separate subspecies, *chioneus*, occurs in the area of the Sixaola River in Limón Province, and south into Panama. The latter subspecies may be encountered quite commonly in Cahuita National Park. The author has at times observed apparent hybrids between this species and *Heliconius melpomene*. These butterflies resemble *Heliconius cydno*, but possess orange patches within the white areas of their forewings.

Females of *Heliconius cydno* lay their eggs upon young growth of their foodplants. The mature larvae have yellow heads, long black spines, and light brown bodies. As is usual with this genus, the pupae are extremely cryptic. They are shaded in brown, and are ornamented with black spines. The butterflies eclose ten to fourteen days after pupation.

● ●

Family:	NYMPHALIDAE
Subfamily:	HELICONIINAE
Species:	*Heliconius erato* Plate 1
Distribution:	This species flies in southern Mexico, and throughout Central America to Brasil. The subspecies *petiverana* occurs in Costa Rica.
Larval foodplants:	Several varieties of *Passiflora* (Passifloraceae) are consumed by the larvae of this species, including *Passiflora biflora* and *Passiflora talamancensis*.
General information:	*Heliconius erato* is a common butterfly that is observed along forest edges and in open areas to elevations of over 1,200 meters throughout Costa Rica. The adults are often seen while taking nectar from *Lantana* flowers, which are common weeds in many of the areas which the butterflies inhabit. This butterfly has a gentle flight, with the shallow wing beats that are typical of its genus, and is instantly recognizable. The larvae are quite easy to find upon their foodplants, and are white with long black spines. Pupae of *Heliconius erato* are brown, and hang by their tails. They are excellently camouflaged, resembling small dried leaves.

● ●

Family:	NYMPHALIDAE
Subfamily:	HELICONIINAE
Species:	*Heliconius hecale* Plate 1
Distribution:	*Heliconius hecale* is widely distributed from southern Mexico to Ecuador and the Amazon. This species is represented by a variety of regional subspecies, with subspecies *zuleika* flying in Costa Rica.
Larval foodplants:	A variety of *Passiflora* species (Passifloraceae), amongst which *Passiflora vitifolia* is a popular choice.
General information:	*Heliconius hecale* is a common member of its genus, and flies in a variety of forest and disturbed habitats throughout Costa Rica, to well over 1,000 meters in elevation. These butterflies are conspicuous gliding fliers, which are often observed while nectaring upon a variety of flowers.

This species exhibits wing colouration and patterning which is typically used by many species of butterflies that are involved in mimicry complexes throughout much of Central and South America. This butterfly emits a pungent odour from glands at the tip of its abdomen if it is bothered.

Larvae of *Heliconius hecale* are quite easily located upon their *Passiflora* foodplants. When mature the larvae are white with black spotting, possess long black spines and have yellowish-orange heads. The pupae are brown, hang by their tails, and closely resemble dried leaves.

• •

Family:	NYMPHALIDAE
Subfamily:	ITHOMIINAE
Species:	*Mechanitis polymnia* Plate 6
Distribution:	This butterfly occurs in southern Mexico and throughout Central America and South America. Subspecies *isthmia* occurs in Costa Rica.
Larval foodplants:	Species of *Solanum* (Solanaceae) are consumed by the larvae of *Mechanitis polymnia*.
General information:	*Mechanitis polymnia* is a familiar Costa Rican species of the subfamily Ithomiinae. It occurs commonly throughout the country in open areas and along forest edges, wherever its larval foodplant *Solanum* grows. *Solanum* belongs to the plant family Solanaceae, species of which contain toxins in their leaf tissues.

These butterflies are slow and conspicuous fliers, which are easily located and observed if present in their habitats. Females of this species, and other Ithomiines, are frequently discovered while feeding upon bird droppings. From the latter food source, they appear to obtain nitrogen, which is utilized for the production of their eggs. A wide variety of flowers are visited for nectar by both sexes.

Females of *Mechanitis polymnia* lay batches of white, skittle-shaped eggs upon the upper surfaces of the hostplant leaves. The larvae grow gregariously, and when mature are green, and possess fleshy tubercles which are positioned laterally along the length of their bodies. Pupae of this butterfly hang by the tail, are coloured in glistening gold, and are extremely beautiful.

• •

Family:	NYMPHALIDAE
Subfamily:	MORPHINAE
Species:	*Morpho cypris* Plate 3
Distribution:	*Morpho cypris* is found from Nicaragua to Ecuador, with the subspecies *schausi* occurring in Costa Rica.
Larval foodplants:	The author has observed this species ovipositing on one occasion upon a large *Inga* tree (Mimosaceae). This is the same foodplant that is indicated by DeVries (1987: 244-245).
General Information:	This spectacular species, which is one of the jewels of the Costa Rican butterfly fauna, occurs commonly in suitable rainforest habitats throughout the country, from low to medium elevations. To view the iridescent blue male as it flies in the morning sunlight is an experience that will never be forgotten.

Individuals of this species become active in the mid-morning, with the greatest amount of activity occurring between eleven o'clock in the morning and one o'clock in the afternoon, when males actively patrol well-lit trails and forest clearings with a strong swooping flight. In the mid-afternoons, the males feed upon fermenting fruits, such as bananas. The author has observed this species upon many occasions at such food sources, which were utilized as lures in order to observe the insects more closely. Individuals which responded to baits seemed to arrive very punctually at half past two in the afternoon.

When not engaged in such feeding behaviours, **Morpho cypris** usually flies at canopy or subcanopy levels, and rarely descends to the ground. The females of this species are encountered very rarely, and occur in two colour forms, these being ochre or blue. The female that the author observed while ovipositing was a blue individual. It laid several eggs upon the foliage of a large *Inga* tree (Mimosaceae) which was growing along the bank of a forest stream.

••

Family:	NYMPHALIDAE
Subfamily:	MORPHINAE
Species:	*Morpho peleides* Plate 3
Distribution:	*Morpho peleides* occurs from Mexico to Ecuador and Venezuela, and is represented on a regional basis by a variety of different subspecies. Subspecies **limpida** and **marinita** fly in Costa Rica.
Larval foodplants:	Many members of the family Fabaceae are utilized as hostplants by larvae of *Morpho peleides*. These include genera such as **Mucuna, Lonchocarpus, Machaerium** and **Pterocarpus**, the latter of which is referred to locally as "Chaperno". These are all woody shrubs and vines which grow abundantly in forests and disturbed habitats from low to medium elevations.
General information:	This is a common Costa Rican species which occurs in forest habitats throughout the country. Its spectacular colouration and sailing, erratic flight make it instantly recognizable. Individuals may be encountered in all months of the year in Costa Rica, and are most often observed in the mornings, while flying along the trails, forest edges and rivers courses of their habitats.

These butterflies feed primarily upon rotting fruits and fermenting fungal growths, and may visit specific food sources repeatedly over the course of several days. While feeding, the wings are held closed, which serves to clearly display the dark colouration and large ocelli upon their undersides, which provide excellent crypsis. Many of these butterflies are observed in nature to possess wing damage, due to attempted predation. Such damage is usually sustained while the butterflies feed at ground level.

Females of **Morpho peleides** usually oviposit during the early afternoons, at which time they may be observed floating gently amongst the vegetation while searching for foodplants along forest edges. When a suitable plant is located, several eggs may be deposited upon the uppersides of its leaves. The ova are green and hemispherical, which serves to conceal them extremely effectively upon the plant. If fertile, a dark line soon develops around the top of the egg, which subsequently hatches in 8 to 10 days. Many of the eggs of this species fall victim to parasitic wasps of the family Trichogrammatidae, which deposit their own eggs inside those of *Morpho peleides* and other butterflies.

Upon hatching, the larvae of this butterfly consume their empty egg shells completely. They then conceal themselves upon the undersides of the leaves of the hostplant between meals. The larvae feed by adhering to a dawn and dusk cycle. This measured feeding pattern seems to increase the time needed to complete their growth. The larvae of *Morpho peleides* often require more than ten weeks to mature fully, which is a considerable period of time compared to that required for larval maturation in most tropical butterfly species.

During the first four instars, the larvae are colored in brown, red and yellow, and are ornamented with colourful tufts of hair. Upon entering the fifth instar, they gradually lose this bright colouration, and develop mottled brown markings. This makes them almost invisible while they rest lengthwise along the woody stems of their hostplants. The head capsules of these larvae are clothed with numerous spiny bristles. These bristles may break off into the skin if the larvae are bothered, often resulting in an irritation.

As the time for pupation approaches, the larvae of *Morpho peleides* lose much of their size, and gradually change colour to become green over the duration of two or three days. Subsequently, they suspend themselves by the tail in order to prepare for pupation. The pupae of *Morpho peleides* are green, almost oval in shape, and hang head downwards from their supports by a brown tail, which gives them the appearance of leaf buds. The butterflies emerge after a pupal stage of approximately three weeks, with eclosion usually taking place during the mid-morning.

Morpho peleides occurs as two different subspecies in Costa Rica, depending upon the region in question. In the Atlantic sector of Costa Rica, and the northwest Pacific zone, the subspecies *limpida* occurs, in which the uppersides of the wings are largely covered in blue with black wing borders. The region of the Central Valley and to the west and south is home to the subspecies *marinita*. *Morpho peleides marinita* is brown in ground colour, and is patterned with very variable and often extremely reduced amounts of blue.

A particularly pleasant area in which to encounter *Morpho peleides* is Cahuita National Park in southern Limón Province, where many individuals of this species may be readily observed while flying along the trail which runs parallel to the beach. Fruits from Almendro trees fall along this trail, and the insects may often be observed while feeding upon them during the afternoon. Individuals of *Morpho peleides* which fly at Cahuita are often extremely large and spectacular.

Family:	NYMPHALIDAE
Subfamily:	MORPHINAE
Species:	*Morpho theseus* Figure 5.2
Distribution:	*Morpho theseus* is widely distributed from southern Mexico to Ecuador. There are many different subspecies of this insect, which vary widely in colouration from grey to blue, green and white depending upon the location in which they occur. Two different subspecies, namely *aquarius* and *gynodela*, fly in Costa Rica.

A   B

Fig 5.2   Two subspecies of *Morpho theseus* that fly in Costa Rica.
A: subspecies *gynodela*;
B: subspecies *aquarius*.

Larval foodplants: The foodplants and early stages of this species are unknown.

General information: This is a common rainforest butterfly which flies from sea level to altitudes of 1,000 meters or more. The reddish-brown underside markings, and brownish-grey colouration of the upperside of its wings make this species very distinctive as it sails along slowly with a alternating gliding and flicking motion. Virtually nothing is known of the ecology of this species. *Morpho theseus aquarius* is particularly common in Braulio Carrillo National Park, where individuals may be readily observed while flying along rivers and around forest clearings. A separate subspecies, *Morpho theseus gynodela*, occurs at medium to higher altitudes in the Talamancan Mountains in the south of Costa Rica, and into the adjacent Chiriquí Province of Panama. This subspecies is slightly smaller than *aquarius*, and is lightly coloured in white, grey and brown, with prominent spotting ornamenting the margins of the uppersides of its wings.

Family:	NYMPHALIDAE
Subfamily:	NYMPHALINAE
Species:	*Adelpha cytherea* Plate 6
Distribution:	*Adelpha cytherea* occurs commonly from southern Mexico to Amazonas, with subspecies *marcia* flying in Costa Rica.
Larval Foodplants:	Females of this species oviposit upon *Sabicea villosa* (Rubiaceae), which is a straggly plant that grows commonly along forest edges.
General information:	This is a very representative Costa Rican species, which occurs commonly in forests and along forest edges. The butterflies are great lovers of fallen fruits, and may often be observed in small groups while feeding in such situations. These insects will remain in close proximity to available food sources for considerable periods of time. The author observed specific individuals returning on a daily basis to feed upon fermenting guayaba fruits in an orchard for the duration of nearly three weeks.

• •

Family:	NYMPHALIDAE
Subfamily:	NYMPHALINAE
Species:	*Anartia fatima* Plate 6
Distribution:	This common butterfly is found from the southern United States to Panama.
Larval foodplants:	Larvae of *Anartia fatima* feed upon common members of the plant family Acanthaceae, such as *Justicia* and *Blechum*.
General information:	This is an abundant insect, which is distributed throughout Costa Rica to altitudes of 1,200 meters or more. The adults are very active fliers that are encountered in open areas and especially locations that have been disturbed by human settlement. In such situations, their weedy hostplants grow in profusion, and the butterflies may be extremely common.

Females of *Anartia fatima* oviposit in strong sunshine, and deposit single, tiny green eggs upon the hostplants. The mature larvae are black, peppered with small white spots, and possess short bristly spines. Their heads are black and glossy, and are adorned with two horns. The pupae of this butterfly are green or brown in colour, and are well hidden within the cover of weedy plants in which the foodplants usually grow.

• •

Family:	NYMPHALIDAE
Subfamily:	NYMPHALINAE
Species:	*Biblis hyperia* Plate 6
Distribution:	This butterfly flies from Mexico to Peru and Amazonas.
Larval foodplants:	According to DeVries (1987: 137), the foodplant of this butterfly is *Tragia volubilis* (Euphorbiaceae).
General Information:	*Biblis hyperia* is most frequently encountered in habitats which have been altered by human activities, and is

71

distributed throughout Costa Rica. This is an extremely distinctive and beautiful butterfly, which is quite unmistakable when observed in flight. The author has frequently encountered this insect in Santa Ana, which lies west of San José. At this locality it may be observed particularly at the onset of the rainy season during May and June. Individuals which fly during the wet season seem to be larger and more robust than those that exist during dryer periods. This butterfly is often observed while drinking at mud puddles, and occasionally feeds upon fermenting fruits.

Family:	NYMPHALIDAE
Subfamily:	NYMPHALINAE
Species:	*Catonephele numilia* Plate 6
Distribution:	This species occurs throughout much of Latin America.
Larval Foodplants:	Species of *Alchornea* (Euphorbiaceae)
General Information:	This butterfly is a resident of the canopies of forests throughout Costa Rica, to elevations of 1,000 meters or more. It is frequently observed after having descended to feed upon mammal dung and fermenting fruits.

Catonephele numilia is very dimorphic with regard to the appearance of the different sexes. The males possess three orange spots upon the black ground colour of the uppersides of their wings, while the females are black with a prominent cream coloured band which runs across each forewing. In addition, the overall shape of male's wings is quite rounded, while the forewings of the female are processed to a prominent tip. The wing undersurfaces of both sexes are cryptically coloured in tan and shades of brown, which serves to conceal these butterflies very effectively while they feed.

Larvae of this species are very similar in structure and habits to those of *Nessaea aglaura*, to which this butterfly is closely related. Likewise, the pupae are green in colour, with brown mottling upon their wingcases. They are held horizontally in relation to the substrates to which they are attached, which are usually leaves.

Family:	NYMPHALIDAE
Subfamily:	NYMPHALINAE
Species:	*Chlosyne janais* Plate 6
Distribution:	From southern Mexico to Ecuador.
Larval foodplants:	Members of the plant family Acanthaceae, of which *Justicia* is a species observed to be frequently utilized by the author.
General information:	This beautiful butterfly is a familiar Costa Rican species that visits many varieties of flowers, such as *Lantana* and *Zinnias*. When in flight, the black and orange colouration of this species makes it very conspicuous and readily identifiable.

Females of *Chlosyne janais* lay large masses of tiny yellow eggs upon the undersurfaces of the hostplant leaves. The resultant larvae develop gregariously, and molt their skins in a synchronized fashion. When mature, the larvae are light yellowish green, and possess black spines. The pupae are also light green, hang by the tail, and are ornamented with black spots. *Chlosyne janais* is a very common and representative species of Costa Rica's butterfly fauna.

• •

Family:	NYMPHALIDAE
Subfamily:	NYMPHALINAE
Species:	*Hamadryas amphinome* Plate 6
Distribution:	This butterfly ranges widely from southern Mexico to Ecuador, Peru and the Amazon. A number of different subspecies exist, with subspecies ***mexicana*** flying in Costa Rica.
Larval foodplants:	The larvae of *Hamadryas amphinome* feed upon varieties of ***Dalechampia***, which are weedy climbers of the plant family Euphorbiaceae.
General information:	*Hamadryas amphinome* is a member of a genus of butterflies that are popularly referred to as "Crackers". This term refers to the crackling sounds that these butterflies produce when they fly. This species is common in forest habitats and adjacent disturbed habitats throughout Costa Rica to altitudes of 1,200 meters or more.

The most usual situation in which to find the butterflies is while they are resting with their heads pointing downwards upon the trunks of trees. The mottled grey and blue colours of their wings blends in very well with this background, providing excellent camouflage. Several individuals may often be observed while resting in this manner upon a single tree trunk, often in the company of other species of *Hamadryas*.

The adults of this butterfly usually feed upon fermenting fruits, and may be easily attracted to this food source if it is used as a bait. The females deposit their eggs upon the hostplants in chains, with each egg being connected to the other in a long hanging row. The resultant larvae develop gregariously, and when mature are black, with yellow markings upon the dorsal surface of their bodies, and are covered with orange and black spines. Pupae of *Hamadryas amphinome* hang head downwards, are brown, and resemble dried leaves.

• •

Family:	NYMPHALIDAE
Subfamily:	NYMPHALINAE
Species:	*Marpesia merops* Plate 6
Distribution:	*Marpesia merops* flies from Central America to Bolivia.
Larval Foodplants:	Unknown to the author.
General Information:	This common butterfly is frequently met with in forests throughout Costa Rica, to altitudes of 2,000 meters or more. The males often congregate while drinking water along river courses and streamsides. One such gathering that the author witnessed at San Gerardo de Dota, in the Talamancan Mountains, consisted of hundreds of individuals.

Family:	NYMPHALIDAE
Subfamily:	NYMPHALINAE
Species:	*Nessaea aglaura* Plate 6
Distribution:	*Nessaea aglaura* is found from Mexico to Colombia.
Larval Foodplants:	This butterfly utilizes ***Alchornea*** trees (Euphorbiaceae) as larval foodplants.
General information:	*Nessaea aglaura* is one of the most beautiful and dramatic of Costa Rica's butterflies. It is unusual with respect to the blue colouration of the upper surfaces of its wings. This is because this colour is the result of pigmentation, and is not structurally produced as is the case of the same colour in most other butterflies. The green underside colouration of this species provides it with extremely effective camouflage, and renders these insects virtually invisible while they perch upon leaves in situations such as forest edges and along streams. The male differs from the female in that it possess an orange patch next to the margin of each hindwing on the upper wing surfaces.

Females of ***Nessaea aglaura*** deposit their eggs singly upon the undersurfaces of the hostplant's leaves. The larvae commence feeding upon the tissues adjacent to the leaf tip, and rest upon the dry brown midrib which remains as a result of this behaviour. This makes the larvae easy to locate by simply examining such leaf tips, as the tiny brown larvae will frequently be discovered while resting upon the ends of these appendages. The mature larvae of this species are bluish-green, and possess extremely long and well armatured orange spines. Their heads are black with a metallic blue luster. There are two long, orange and blue horns which arise from the head capsule, both of which bristle with long spines. While at rest upon the uppersurfaces of the hostplant's leaves, the larvae of this butterfly are virtually invisible. Their long spines effectively blur the outlines of their bodies, which serves to effectively blend them into the background colouration of the leaves upon which they are situated. The green and brown pupa of ***Nessaea aglaura*** is attached by the tail to the uppersurface of a leaf, and is held in a horizontal manner to the leaf in question (Fig. 3.5).

The food sources of these butterflies include dung and fermenting fruits. This species is usually encountered as solitary individuals. However, the author has occasionally observed it in larger numbers within suitable habitats, particularly in the Atlantic lowlands.

Family: NYMPHALIDAE
Subfamily: NYMPHALINAE
Species: *Siproeta epaphus*   Figure 5.3
Distribution: From Mexico to Bolivia.

Fig 5.3   A freshly emerged adult of *Siproeta epaphus* (Nymphalinae).

Larval foodplants: Representatives of the plant family Acanthaceae, with some favourites being *Justicia* and *Blechum* being preferred hosts.

General information: Although generally not as common as its close relative *Siproeta steneles*, this species is still a familiar and distinctive butterfly of forest edges throughout much of Costa Rica.

The adults are most frequently observed while flying strongly and gracefully along the edges of their habitats, especially the females, which actively search for foodplants in such situations when there is direct sun. As is the case with *Siproeta steneles*, this butterfly utilizes a wide variety of food sources, including flower nectar and juices from fermenting fruits.

This butterfly lays small, green, barrel shaped eggs upon young growth of the chosen hostplants. The mature larva of this species possesses orange-tipped yellow spines, and is purplish-black in colour. Its black head capsule is crowned with two long, bristly, orange horns. The ovoid, jade green pupa of *Siproeta epaphus* hangs by the tail, and is finely dotted with black upon its abdominal segments. Two pairs of short, maroon-tipped yellow spines arise from the dorsal mid-section of the pupa.

• •

Family: NYMPHALIDAE
Subfamily: NYMPHALINAE
Species: *Siproeta steneles*   Plate 6
Distribution: *Siproeta steneles* ranges from the southern United States, to the Caribbean, Mexico, Central America to Brazil. Subspecies *biplagiata* is found in Costa Rica.

Larval foodplants: Species of the plant family Acanthaceae are utilized by *Siproeta steneles*, including *Justicia* and *Blechum*.

General information: This beautiful and familiar species, which is popularly referred to as "The Malachite", is distributed throughout Costa Rica in forest and disturbed habitats to elevations of 1,200 meters or more. The lovely lime green colouration of this species gradually fades to a dull yellow upon exposure to sunlight, but its patterning and wing shape are very distinctive. These butterflies are very liberal regarding their choices of food sources, which may include fermenting fruits, animal dung, and nectar from a variety of flowers. The adults are most frequently observed along the edges of forests and within wooded areas, and are strong, sailing fliers. They are very well camouflaged whilst at rest along shaded forest edges, and may be quite difficult to detect in such situations. This species may be very abundant, especially during the commencement of the rainy season in the Central Valley. At this time, numerous individuals may be observed while feeding upon fallen fruits such as guayaba.

Usually, the females oviposit upon the young growth of the chosen foodplants. The mature larvae are charcoal coloured, and are covered with long, reddish spines. Pupae of *Siproeta steneles* hang by their tails, are green, ovoid, and marked delicately with black spotting upon their abdomens.

• •

Family: NYMPHALIDAE
Subfamily: SATYRINAE
Species: *Cithaerias menander*   Plate 4
Distribution: This butterfly is found from Mexico to Ecuador.
Larval foodplants: Unknown to the author.
General information: This is one of the most precious and delicate insects in the world, and is a familiar component of tropical forest habitats in Costa Rica. These butterflies sail like ghosts over the forest floor, with only the luminous pink patches on their wings betraying their presence. When perched upon low vegetation, they may be seen to possess totally transparent wings, excepting the pink areas and delicate ocelli of the hindwings. This species can be quite common, especially if fermenting palm fruits are present, as these are a favourite food of the adults. *Cithaerias menander* occurs in rainforests throughout Costa Rica, to altitudes of 1,800 meters or more.

• •

Family: NYMPHALIDAE
Subfamily: SATYRINAE
Species: *Manataria maculata*   Plate 4
Distribution: This species flies from southern Mexico to Brasil.
Larval foodplants: Bamboo (Poaceae)(DeVries 1987: 264).

General Information:	The author has observed this species quite commonly in the Central Valley between the months of August and October, but it is also common at other times along the Pacific side of the country. These insects are very swift and powerful fliers, which frequent fermenting fruits, such as guayaba. While at rest upon tree trunks and branches, as is their usual habit, these butterflies are extremely well camouflaged.

- -

Family:	NYMPHALIDAE
Subfamily:	SATYRINAE
Species:	*Pierella helvetica* Plate 4
Distribution:	This species flies from Mexico to Ecuador as several subspecies. In Costa Rica, subspecies *incanescens* occurs.
Larval foodplants:	The larvae of *Pierella helvetica* feed upon several species of *Heliconia* (Heliconiaceae).
General information:	This common forest species is readily observed while sailing delicately along the ground, and in and out of low vegetation within its habitats. It occurs throughout Costa Rica to elevations of 1,000 meters or more. The habits of this insect are very similar to those of *Pierella luna*, but this butterfly seems to be more abundant in relation to the former species.

Females of *Pierella helvetica* oviposit upon the leaves and stems of *Heliconia* plants, especially younger specimens. The larvae are extremely similar to those of *Pierella luna*, but are darker brown in colour. The pupa is brown, compact, and formed near the ground upon the foodplant, or on nearby vegetation.

- -

Family:	NYMPHALIDAE
Subfamily:	SATYRINAE
Species:	*Pierella luna* Plate 4
Distribution:	*Pierella luna* is found from Mexico to Ecuador. Subspecies *luna* flies in Costa Rica.
Larval foodplants:	Several species of *Heliconia* (Heliconiaceae) are used by this butterfly as larval hostplants.
General information:	This butterfly is common in forest habitats throughout the country, where it may be observed while gliding in a very controlled manner across the forest floor. Occasionally, individuals may be encountered while perching upon leaves on the ground that are illuminated by patches of sunlight. While engaging in this behaviour, the white spots upon the hindwings are often displayed.

These butterflies feed upon a variety of fermenting fruits, and sometimes upon fermenting fungal growths. Females have been observed by the author while ovipositing upon many varieties of *Heliconia* plants. The round, white eggs are quite large for the size of the butterfly. They are usually deposited upon the undersurfaces of the hostplant's leaves, but sometimes on the stems.

Mature larvae of **Pierella luna** are brown, but may often possess green colouration blended into the ground colour. They are smooth in texture, and have small bumps upon their head capsules. Usually, the larvae conceal themselves at the base of their hostplants when not feeding. Frequently, they become slightly caked with soil as a result of rain splashing it upon them whilst they rest near the ground. The pupae are compact, dark brown, and hang head downwards from the foodplant, or upon adjacent vegetation. These butterflies seem to be quite long lived, as the author has observed the same individuals flying in localized areas of forests for several weeks at a time.

• •

Family:	PAPILIONIDAE
Subfamily:	PAPILIONINAE
Species:	*Battus polydamas* Plate 5
Distribution:	*Battus polydamas* is a resident species of the southern United States, the Caribbean and much of Latin America. Whilst the subspecies which flies throughout the Americas is very consistent in appearance, numerous subspecies have evolved on many of the Caribbean islands. Subspecies *polydamas* occurs throughout much of Costa Rica.
Larval foodplants:	Although it may possibly utilize a variety of species of *Aristolochia* vines (Aristolochiaceae), the author has discovered larvae of this butterfly feeding upon *Aristolochia veraguensis*. *Aristolochia* is known as "Canastilla" in Costa Rica. Canastilla, which means "little basket" in Spanish, refers to the seed pods of these vines, which open into a basket shaped structure upon maturity, in order to dispense their seeds.
General information:	This strong flying butterfly is commonly encountered in a variety of habitats in Costa Rica, but is usually most abundant in association with disturbed habitats. It also occurs in rainforests, where the butterflies feed upon flowers such as Lantana and Verbena along forest edges. The author has observed the same butterflies returning to specific flower patches in order to feed upon several consecutive days.

The small, yellowish-orange eggs are deposited in clusters upon the young leaves of the hostplants, and occasionally on adjacent vegetation. The resultant larvae are gregarious throughout most of their development. Upon maturity, the larvae of this species are light brown in ground colour. They possess brownish or red fleshy tubercles, and their heads are shiny black. The colouration of the mature larvae of **Battus polydamas** provides excellent crypsis while individuals are at rest upon the woody stems of their foodplants. Many of the hostplants which are utilized by the larvae of this species are quite small in size. As a result, the larvae often exhaust their available food supply, and are frequently discovered while wandering across the ground in search of new plants. The pupae of **Battus polydamas** are very flattened in appearance and are brown, or sometimes mottled in green and yellow (Fig. 3.8). Emergence of the adults takes place after a pupal period of 14 to 20 days.

Family: PAPILIONIDAE
Subfamily: PAPILIONINAE
Species: *Papilio anchisiades*   Plate 5
Distribution: *Papilio anchisiades* flies from the southern United States to Amazonia in several subspecies. The subspecies *idaeus* flies in Costa Rica.
Larval foodplants: A variety of cultivated and wild members of the Citrus family (Rutaceae) are consumed by the larvae of this species.
General information: This familiar member of the Papilionidae is a common Costa Rican butterfly, and may be encountered throughout the country from sea level to elevations of over 1,000 meters. It seems to prefer habitats which have been affected by human development, where the Citrus hostplants of the larvae are planted or grow wild, and is often observed even in the center of San José. The strong flying butterflies are avid nectar feeders, which flutter and swoop gracefully from flower to flower. This species is an extremely effective mimic of the females of toxic *Parides* swallowtails, and shares almost identical colouration and patterning as individuals of that genus.

Females of *Papilio anchisiades* deposit their eggs in large clusters. The eggs, which are usually discovered upon the young, tender leaves of the hostplants, are orange and quite conspicuous. The resultant larvae are highly gregarious in all of their instars, and may be located quite readily while they are clustered tightly in large congregations at the bases of the trees upon which they are feeding. When maturity is reached, the larvae are brown with mottled white markings, and are very well camouflaged. As is usual with most species of the genus *Papilio*, the pupae are brown, sticklike, and are sometimes patterned with green markings which resemble lichens. This consequently renders them with excellent camouflage upon their supports, which are usually the twigs and branches of the hostplant, or those of adjacent trees and shrubs.

••

Family: PAPILIONIDAE
Subfamily: PAPILIONINAE
Species: *Papilio garamas*   Figure 5.4
Distribution: *Papilio garamas* occurs from Mexico to Panama, and is represented by a number of distinctive subspecies. In Costa Rica, the subspecies *syedra* flies in cloud forest habitats above 1,000 meters in elevation.

Fig. 5.4   The spectacular Garamas Swallowtail (Papilio garamas syedra) at rest in the cloud forests of Cerro de la Muerte, San José province.

Larval foodplants: Unknown to the author.

General information: Although not abundant in Costa Rica, with perseverance and a good pair of binoculars, it is possible to observe this species as it sails gracefully around the tops of the tallest trees in its cloud forest habitats. This spectacular butterfly cannot be mistaken for any other species where it flies, and is breathtaking to view in nature.

The forests of the Talamancan Mountains which surround the community of San Gerardo de Dota are excellent places in which to search for this butterfly. If located, individuals may be observed for long periods of time while they circle periodically around their high treetop perches. Occasionally, the butterflies descend to take nectar from flowers. The males will also drink water from puddles at stream and river edges. A journey made in order to locate this species will be a memorable one even if this butterfly is not encountered. The Costa Rican cloud forests abound with diverse and fascinating wildlife, including birds such as the breathtaking Resplendent Quetzal.

• •

Family: PAPILIONIDAE

Subfamily: PAPILIONINAE

Species: *Parides iphidamas*   Plate 5

Distribution: *Parides iphidamas* is represented by several subspecies from Mexico to Colombia. In Costa Rica, subspecies *iphidamas* occurs.

Larval foodplants: Several species of *Aristolochia* vines (Aristolochiaceae) are utilized by this species as larval hosts.

General information: *Parides iphidamas* is a common member of its genus in Costa Rica, and flies in forests from sea level to altitudes of over 1,000 meters. It may be observed as readily in the rainforests of the Atlantic lowlands as in wooded habitats surrounding the Central Valley. The butterflies visit a variety of flowers, in particular *Lantana* and *Impatiens*. The females are very conspicuous while searching for *Aristolochia* vines along forest edges. Both sexes appear to prefer shaded conditions in which to fly, as opposed to strong sunlight.

The author has observed females of this species ovipositing upon *Aristolochia pilosa* and *Aristolochia constricta* during the early afternoons. The eggs are purple upon being laid, and are covered with a golden coating which affixes them firmly to the chosen leaf. Young larvae of this species conceal themselves under the leaves of their hostplants, and are more evident upon the vines as they mature and feed more openly. The mature larvae of this butterfly are deep maroon in colour, with whitish-yellow markings along the mid-dorsal sections of their bodies. They are covered in fleshy tubercles, some of which are white, and have shiny black heads. The pupae are held upright by a silken girdle around the body, and are coloured in shades of light green and yellow. They are quite flattened in appearance, and closely resemble dried leaves. Pupae of this and other species of *Parides* will be observed to produce a strong, noxious odour upon close examination.

Family:	PIERIDAE
Subfamily:	COLIADINAE
Species:	*Phoebis philea* Plate 5
Distribution:	*Phoebis philea* occurs on several Caribbean islands, and from Mexico to South America, with subspecies *philea* occurring in Costa Rica.
Larval foodplants:	Females of Phoebis philea oviposit upon a variety of species of *Cassia* (Caesalpinaceae), which grow as abundant shrubs and trees throughout Costa Rica.
General information:	This beautiful yellow and orange butterfly occurs commonly to 1,000 meters or more in elevation throughout Costa Rica, and is a conspicuous and fast flying species. The butterflies nectar upon a variety of flowers, especially red species, such as Hibiscus and Bougainvilleas. The females are often coloured richly with red upon the margins of their hindwings, which is a striking compliment to the their yellow ground colour. These butterflies seem to enjoy hot weather, and are commonly observed whilst swooping strongly around a variety of flowering trees, and while flying across open spaces.

The females oviposit whenever there is strong sun, and frequently leave several eggs upon the same *Cassia* plant. Larvae of *Phoebis philea* are green with orange mottling, and are well hidden upon their hostplants. The pupae of this species are brownish-red or green, have large wing cases, and are supported by silken girdles around their bodies.

· ·

Family:	PIERIDAE
Subfamily:	COLIADINAE
Species:	*Phoebis sennae* Plate 5
Distribution:	The range of *Phoebis sennae* stretches from the southern United States to Mexico, and much of South America.
Larval foodplants:	The larvae feed upon a variety of species of *Cassia* (Caesalpinaceae).
General information:	This abundant species occurs throughout Costa Rica to altitudes of up to 1,000 meters or more. It is a common sight even in cities, where the larval foodplants often grow on vacant land. As is the usual case with the genus *Phoebis*, these butterflies are strong fliers, and visit a wide variety of flowers.

· ·

Family:	PIERIDAE
Subfamily:	DISMORPHIINAE
Species:	*Dismorphia amphione* Plate 5
Distribution:	Southern Mexico and most of Central and South America. Subspecies *praxinoe* flies in Costa Rica.
Larval Hostplants:	A variety of species of *Inga* (Mimosaceae).
General information:	This species is a superb mimic of butterflies of the subfamily Ithomiinae, with which it co-exists, but at much lower levels of population than its models. In particular, the

females are commonly met with along forest edges while searching for their hostplants. In flight behaviour and colouration, they are very convincing copies of Ithomiine species such as the common *Mechanitis polymnia*.

These butterflies lay their eggs singly upon each leaf, but may deposit several eggs upon the same plant. The larvae are green, long and thin, and are highly cannibalistic. If two meet, the younger specimen will invariably perish due to bites delivered by its older competitor. This behaviour may be of survival value, as occasionally the larvae develop upon small plants which may not be capable of sustaining two or more individuals to maturity. The pupae are also green, quite slim, and slightly thicker in the area of the wing cases. Eclosion of the adults takes place after a pupal period of fifteen to twenty days. This butterfly occurs throughout Costa Rica in suitable forest habitats.

• •

Family:	PIERIDAE
Subfamily:	PIERINAE
Species:	*Ascia monuste* Plate 5
Distribution:	From the southern United States to Mexico, Central America and much of South America.
Larval foodplants:	Popular larval hosts for this species include cultivated *Brassicas* (Brassicaceae).
General information:	*Ascia monuste* is a very common and familiar butterfly that flies throughout Costa Rica to altitudes of 1,200 meters or more. The females are frequently observed whilst ovipositing, even in downtown San José. Eggs of *Ascia monuste* are white, skittle-shaped, and although laid singly, several may be deposited upon the same plant. Mature larvae of this species are light green with black markings, and are well hidden upon their foodplants. Both sexes visit the flowers of a great variety of weeds.

• •

Family:	PIERIDAE
Subfamily:	PIERINAE
Species:	*Catasticta teutila* Plate 5
Distribution:	This butterfly is found from Mexico to Colombia as different subspecies. The Costa Rican subspecies is named *flavomaculata*.
Larval foodplants:	The author has discovered larvae of this species feeding gregariously upon an undetermined species of Mistletoe (Loranthaceae), which was growing upon Oak trees at San Gerardo de Dota in San José Province.
General information:	This species is common in hilly country and mountains above 800 meters in elevation. The butterflies may frequently be observed in numbers of one hundred or more whilst drinking at water seepages, and along river banks. They are often extremely enthusiastic while engaging in this behaviour, and may virtually submerge themselves at times in strong running water.

This common butterfly is a fascinating little creature, whose habits make it easy to observe closely. It may often be found drinking with the more uncommon *Catasticta* species, or in the company of many other varieties of butterflies at water sources. Despite their bright colouration when inspected closely, they are quite inconspicuous while congregated in such situations, and often betray themselves only when they are disturbed by an observer walking past them. While in flight, the males display a strong blue iridescence, and are quite conspicuous. The females, which are coloured in orange and black, are likewise easy to identify in flight. Females are often observed whilst being courted by males, which respond strongly to the visual cue of their bright colouration. Both sexes take nectar from a variety of flowers, which include many common weeds.

The larvae of *Catasticta teutila* are highly gregarious. When mature, they are brown and green in colour, with long white hairs upon their bodies, and have shiny black heads. The pupae are green and black with white spotting, and are usually found in groups.

CHAPTER VI

BUTTERFLY FARMING IN COSTA RICA

During the past several years, there has been a great increase in the number of live butterfly exhibits which now span the globe. Although this trend began in Europe decades ago, many countries now boast beautiful tropical butterfly houses, which provide the public with the opportunity of enjoying these creatures at close quarters. Butterfly houses also serve the very useful purpose of educating their visitors about the biology and environmental importance of butterflies. For many people, an exhibit of the type mentioned above may be the closest that one may get to observing live tropical butterflies.

For many years, Costa Rica has been an important source of the live butterfly pupae that are utilized for the purposes of tropical butterfly houses. Throughout Costa Rica, there exists an organized and efficient network of butterfly farmers who raise butterflies in enclosures that they have constructed on their properties. The pupae of the butterflies which they breed are sold to centralized businesses, which subsequently export them to overseas customers. The most established of the latter businesses in Costa Rica is The Butterfly Farm, which distributes tens of thousands of pupae to foreign markets on a yearly basis. Located in La Guácima, near the city of Alajuela, The Butterfly Farm also instructs resident breeders with regard to the effective cultivation of host plants, the prevention of problems in connection with parasites, and other factors which may serve to limit the effectiveness of their efforts. The environmentally friendly practice of composting the plant refuse which may be accumulated while breeding butterflies in large quantities is also actively encouraged.

Costa Rican butterfly farmers usually breed their insects in simple square or rectangular enclosures, which are covered with a fine, black, nylon mesh. The correct hostplants and nectar sources are planted inside, and are permitted to take hold before the butterflies are introduced to breed. It is a remarkably simple matter to cultivate a great variety of species in such simple conditions. Species of **Caligo, Morpho peleides, Heliconius** and **Siproetas** are all butterflies which fare extremely well in captivity, even when confined within relatively small enclosures. Depending upon the ambition and resourcefulness of the individual breeder, more desirable and valuable species may eventually be raised in order to generate improved revenue. Costa Rican butterfly farmers collectively supply over sixty species of butterflies for sale on a regular basis, and many other varieties as they occasionally become available.

Butterfly farmers do not only reside in the wilds of Costa Rica. Many also engage in their activities within suburban areas. Such is the case of María Barbara Escalante who lives on the East side of San José. María breeds a variety of butterflies within her garden enclosure for nearly three years. Her project has also spilled over in order to provide a fascinating activity for the children of the school at which she teaches to participate in. The students manage their own butterfly rearing operation, which is located at their school. This provides the children with an excellent practical learning experience with nature, and also enables them to appreciate that commercial enterprises such as butterfly farming may be engaged in without unduly endangering the environment. Many more butterflies survive in captive situations, where they are better protected from their natural enemies, than could ever do so in nature.

In the community of Monteverde, which is located in the Tilarán Mountains of Puntarenas Province, there is a live butterfly exhibit that is tailored to those who wish to learn more about the habits and ecology of butterflies that exist within a specific environment in Costa Rica.

The Monteverde Butterfly Garden was founded by Jim Wolfe in 1991, as a means by which the cloud forest ecosystem could be interpreted to the public by the butterflies which inhabit it. There are separate enclosures utilized at this butterfly garden, which contain butterfly species that are typical of different elevations and environments within the Tilarán ecosystem. Up to fifty local species of butterflies are bred there, and possibly more when a third enclosure is eventually completed. Included within daily tours is an informative presentation which is given by a guide. The latter activity provides much useful information for the visitor relating to the butterflies and other insects of the Monteverde region.

The exhibit in Monteverde provides one with an ideal opportunity of observing a variety of species of Glasswing butterflies (Ithomiinae), which breed and engage in many of their interesting behaviours there. One may also photograph *Morpho* butterflies and their unusual larvae at close quarters. Leaf mimicking butterflies, such as *Consul electra* fly in the enclosures, as well as other species which are typical of higher elevations, such as *Heliconius clysonymus*. Positions are also available for interested individuals who wish to volunteer their time as guides, in return for room and board.

GLOSSARY

Antennae:

Two segmented organs, situated upon an insects head, that provide balance during flight and also perform sensory functions, such as detecting pheromones.

Androconia:

Specialized scales situated upon the wing surfaces and abdomens of butterflies, which produce chemical scents.

Aposematic:

Conspicuous colouration which serves to convey a warning to potential predators.

Batesian Mimic:

An edible butterfly which gains possible protection from predation by possessing colouration which is very similar to that of another species of butterfly which is toxic.

Claspers:

Two plate shaped organs situated at the tip of the abdomen of a male butterfly, that are utilized to grip the female during mating.

Cremaster:

The hook-tipped terminal abdominal segment of the pupa, which firmly attaches the pupa to its silken substrate.

Extra-floral nectaries:

Structures located upon the stems and other parts of plants, which produce sugary secretions that are attractive to ants and other insects as a food source.

Ecdysis:

The replacement of the skin of a butterfly larva, providing a larger one which permits further development.

Foodplants:

The specific plants utilized by the butterfly in order to complete its larval development.

Forewings:

The pair of wings of a butterfly which are situated adjacently to the head of the insect.

Genus:

A distinctive group of related organisms.

Head capsule:

    The head of a butterfly larva.

Hindwings:

    The pair of wings of a butterfly which are situated adjacently to the abdomen.

Hostplants:

    See foodplants.

Larva (or caterpillar):

    The second stage in the development of a butterfly.

Lek:

    An assembly area where organisms gather in order to engage in courtship displays and behaviours.

Mandibles:

    The hardened larval mouthparts.

Metamorphosis:

    The entire life-cycle of a butterfly, which is comprised of the egg, larva, pupa and adult.

Mullerian mimic:

    A toxic species of butterfly which mimics other toxic butterflies in order to gain protection from predation.

Occelli (or eye-spots):

    Round markings upon the wings of butterflies which closely resemble eyes.

Osmaterium:

    An eversable, forked organ, which larvae of the family Papilionidae possess.

Ovum (or egg):

    The egg of a butterfly.

Ovipositor:

    An organ situated at the tip of the abdomen of a female butterfly, through which fertilized eggs are deposited.

Pheromones:

    Chemical aphrodisiacs that are released from specialized scales possessed by male butterflies during courtship.

Pupa (or chrysalis):

    The immobile third stage of metamorphosis, during which the larval tissues are replaced in order to form the butterfly.

Prolegs:

> The fleshy, sucker-tipped feet of a butterfly larva, which provide it with locomotion.

Scales:

> The minute shingle or hair-like structures present upon butterflies, which provide their colours and textures.

Spiracles:

> Tiny holes through which the larva, pupa and butterfly breathe.

Subfamily:

> A grouping of distinctive species within a particular family of butterflies.

CHECKLIST

Family: NYMPHALIDAE

Subfamily: BRASSOLINAE

Species: *Caligo atreus dionysos* . . . . ❏

              Caligo eurilochus sulanus . . . . ❏

              Caligo memnon memnon . . . . ❏

              Opsiphanes cassina fabricii . . . . ❏

Subfamily: CHARAXINAE

Species: *Prepona omphale octavia* . . . . ❏

Subfamily: DANAINAE

Species: *Danaus plexippus* . . . . ❏

              Lycorea cleobaea atergatis . . . . ❏

Subfamily: HELICONIINAE

Species: *Dryas iulia iulia* . . . . ❏

              Eueides aliphera aliphera . . . . ❏

              Heliconius charitonius charitonius . . . . . . ❏

              Heliconius cydno galanthus . . . . ❏

              Heliconius erato petiverana . . . . ❏

              Heliconius hecale zuleika . . . . ❏

Subfamily: ITHOMIINAE

Species: *Mechanitis polymnia isthmia* . . . . ❏

Subfamily: MORPHINAE

Species: *Morpho cypris schausi* . . . . ❏

              Morpho peleides limpida . . . . ❏

              Morpho peleides marinita . . . . ❏

Morpho theseus aquarius . . . . ❑

Morpho theseus gynodela . . . . ❑

Subfamily: NYMPHALINAE

Species: *Adelpha cytherea marcia* . . . . ❑

Anartia fatima . . . . ❑

Biblis hyperia . . . . ❑

Catonephele numila esite . . . . ❑

Chlosyne janais janais . . . . ❑

Hamadryas amphinome mexicana . . . . . . ❑

Marpesia merops . . . . ❑

Nessaea aglaura aglaura . . . . ❑

Siproeta epaphus epaphus . . . . ❑

Siproeta steneles biplagiata . . . . ❑

Subfamily: SATYRINAE

Species: *Cithaerias menander menander* . . . . ❑

Manataria maculata maculata . . . . ❑

Pierella helvetica incanescens . . . . ❑

Pierella luna luna . . . . ❑

Family: PAPILIONIDAE

Subfamily: PAPILIONINAE

Tribe: PAPILIONINI

Species: *Papilio anchisiades idaeus* . . . . ❏

Papilio garamas syedra . . . . ❏

Tribe: TROIDINI

Species: *Battus polydamas polydamas* . . . . ❏

Parides iphidamas iphidamas . . . . ❏

Family: PIERIDAE

Subfamily: COLIADINAE

Species: *Phoebis philea philea* . . . . ❏

Phoebis sennae sennae . . . . ❏

Subfamily: DISMORPHIINAE

Species: *Dismorphia amphione praxinoe* . . . . ❏

Subfamily: PIERINAE

Species: *Ascia monuste monuste* . . . . ❏

Catasticta teutila flavomaculata . . . . ❏

BIBLIOGRAPHY

Ackery, P.R., and R.I. Vane-Wright
> 1984   *Milkweed Butterflies: Their Cladistics and Biology*. British Museum (Natura History), Entomology: London.

Barcant, M.
> 1970   *Butterflies of Trinidad and Tobago*. Collins: London.

Benson, W.W.
> 1972   Natural Selection for Mullerian Mimicry in *Heliconius erato* in Costa Rica. *Science* 1976:936-939.

D'Abrera, B.
> 1981   *Butterflies of the Neotropical Region, Part I. Papilionidae and Pieridae*. Lansdowne: Melbourne.

> 1984   *Butterflies of the Neotropical Region, Part II. Danainae, Ithomiidae, Heliconidae and Morphidae*. Hill House: Victoria.

DeVries, P.J.
> 1987   *The Butterflies of Costa Rica and Their Natural History: Papilionidae, Pieridae, Nymphalidae*. Princeton University Press: New Jersey.

Emsley, M.
> 1963   A Morphological Study of Imagine Heliconiinae (Lep.: Nymphalidae) with the Consideration of the Evolutionary Relationships within the Group. *Zoologica* N.Y. 48:85-130.

> 1964   The Geographical Distribution of the Color Pattern Components of *Heliconius erato* and *Heliconius melpomene* with Genetical Evidence for the Systematic Relationships between the two Species. *Zoologica* N.Y. 49:245-286.

Gilbert, L.E.
> 1972   Pollen Feeding and Reproductive Biology of *Heliconius* Butterflies. *Proc. Nat. Acad. Sci.* 69:1403-1407.

Goode, M.
> 1988   *Field notes*
> 1989   *Field notes*
> 1998   *Field notes*

LeMoult, E., and R. Real
> 1962   Les Morpho d'Amerique de Sud et Centrale. *Novit. ent.* (*Suppl.*):1-296.

Smiley, J.T.
> 1978   Plant Chemistry and the Evolution of Host Specificity: New Evidence from *Heliconius* and *Passiflora*. *Science* 201:745-747.

Young, A.M.
> 1982   Notes on the Natural History of *Morpho granadensis polybaptus* Butler (Lepidoptera: Nymphalidae: Morphinae) and its Relation to that of *Morpho peleides limpida* Butler. *J.N.Y. Entomol. Soc.* 90:35-54.

Young, A.M., and A. Muyshondt
> 1973   The Biology of *Morpho peleides* in Central America. *Caribb. J. Sci.* 13:1-49.

INDEX

NOTES

NOTES

NOTES